Tropical Gardening Along the Gulf Coast

Gerald K. Arp

Pacesetter Press
A Division of Gulf Publishing Company
Houston, Texas

Illustrated by Terry J. Moore

Tropical Gardening Along the Gulf Coast

Copyright © 1978 by Gulf Publishing Company, Houston, Texas. All rights reserved. Printed in the United States of America. This book, or parts thereof, may not be reproduced in any form without permission of the publisher.

Library of Congress Catalog Card Number 78-53815

ISBN 0-88415-883-7

Edited by B.J. Lowe
Designed by Darlene Crane

Back cover photograph courtesy of *Houston Home and Garden* magazine

Preface

Tropical Gardening Along the Gulf Coast is a companion to *Southern Lawns and Groundcovers, Herb Gardening in the South,* and other books in the Pacesetter Press southern gardening series. As with each of these other books, the effort is directed to resolving some of the peculiar and persisting problems southern gardeners encounter when dealing with our Gulf Coast climate and soils.

Tropical Gardening Along the Gulf Coast does differ from traditional gardening books. In this book I shall emphasize a variety of little utilized ideas and tropical garden subjects that can add a new and exotic dimension to the typical southern garden. My special concerns are the choice and handling of tropical and exotic plants for use in our gardens. I have discussed garden structures, paths, bridges, etc.; these topics are covered nicely elsewhere in greater detail. But there are many fine, little known plants to be grown; my desire is to acquaint you with them.

The book is devoted to raising tropical plants in zones 8 and 9 of USDA Plant Hardiness map; it will be especially useful in the area within 200 miles of the Gulf Coast. It also covers some portions further inland and parts of the South Atlantic seaboard from South Carolina to northern Florida.

Our region is typified by hot, sultry summers and cool wet winters. Summers are usually 90° or more and last from late May to late September. Winter is wet and cool with some freezing weather, but seldom below 28°. Occasionally, winter temperatures will drop to 20° for short periods; prolonged freezes are quite rare, and the ground never freezes. Rainfall is common and averages 3 to 4 inches per month all year. As you will see later, droughts can be a problem but they seldom persist.

The first chapter deals with what constitutes a tropical place, how the Gulf area compares to it, and how it differs. From this discussion you will be able to see what you need to do to create a tropical effect with reasonable success.

The next chapter will be devoted to general cultivation of a tropical garden. The problems section is specifically designed to show how to get tropicals through difficult times of frost, droughts, etc. Ways to put together tropical gardens, atriums, and patios are also covered.

The rest of the book is devoted to specific plants for the garden. Here you'll find descriptions of a wide assortment of tropical plants as well as many interesting ideas and suggestions. You will also see how incredibly diverse the group of plants for the tropical garden is.

A series of special feature sections are included to provide details, commentaries or information on interesting facets of particular garden plants, problems, and ideas.

I think *Tropical Gardening Along the Gulf Coast* will provide a source of interesting new ideas for southern gardeners and that it will add a new dimension to your gardening library.

Acknowledgments

Writing a book on any subject is never done solely by one person. For an author to successfully complete his task he must draw upon the assistance of a variety of people, and this book is no exception. As with many tasks, this effort found itself quite short of time, yet everyone involved accommodated my schedule very graciously.

The entire project would have been hopeless were it not for the kindness of many gardeners and nurserymen in allowing me free access to their gardens. Photographs of many plants were taken in the gardens of: Mr. and Mrs. Forrest of the Forrest Nursery in Friendswood, Texas; Mr. and Mrs. Alan Schott of Groves Exotica Nursery in Houston, Texas; Ken Townsend, "The Greenhouse," also in Houston; Mr. Hines Poth; Mr. and Mrs. Sam Chism; Mr. Bill Wolter; Mr. and Mrs. Erwin Ruhland; and Dr. and Mrs. Alberto Broce.

Mr. Ron Davis, of Houston, provided excellent photographic support, especially in some of the darker gardens; without his help many fine garden plants would not have been included.

The maps on pages 1, 5, and 6 are from *The Climatic Atlas of the United States*, Environmental Science Services Administration, U.S. Dept. of Commerce, 1968.

Ms. Sandy Wilkinson did an outstanding job of typing this manuscript from my rather "distinctive" handwriting. When time became crucial, Ms. Mary Kaye Porter provided able typing assistance.

Ms. Bronwyn Owens contributed immeasurable moral support and somehow managed to smile through the long hours needed to complete this effort.

I also thank my parents, Mr. and Mrs. William Arp of Golden, Colorado.

Contents

Preface, iii

A Look at the Tropics and the Gulf Coast, 1

What Makes a Tropical Place Tropical?, 1; Where are the Tropics?, 1; What are the Tropics Like?, 2; Some Variations on a Tropical Theme, 2; The Montane Rain Forest, 2; The Cloud Forest, 3; The Tropical Deciduous Forest, 3; Confusing Non-Tropical Places, 4; A Look at the Gulf Coast, 4; How Gulf Coast Seasons Resemble Tropical Seasons, 5; Seasonal Variations That Can Cause Problems, 7; Droughts, 7; Hard Freezes, 7; Why We Have These Peculiar Weather Problems, 7; What Does All This Mean?, 8.

How to Care for Your Tropical Garden, 9

Soil Preparation, 9; Humus, 10; Water, 10; Fertilizer, 11; Soil pH, 11; Preparing the Beds, 11; Spacing, 11; Pests, 12; Insects, 12; Diseases, 13; Propagation, 13; Division, 13; Cuttings, 14; Runners, 14; Seeds, 14; Layering, 15; Special Techniques for Tropical Plant Survival, 16; Cold, 16; Rain, 17; Heat, 20; Drought, 20.

Putting Your Tropical Garden Together, 22

How to Begin, 22; Location, 22; Plans, 23; Landscaping with Tropical Plants, 23; Gardens, 23; Protected Entryways, 25; Atriums, 25; Patios and Planters, 27; Swimming Pools, 28; Garden Pools, 29; Pathways, 29; Walls, Screens and Fences, 32; Bridges, 32; Furniture, 32; Lighting, 32; Focal Points, 32.

Tropical Plants for the Gulf Coast, 33

Acalypha wilkesiana, 33
Adiantum capillus—veneris, 33
Agapanthus sp., 34
Agave sp., 34
Albizzia julibrissin, 35
Allamanda cathartica, 35
Aloe vera, 35
Alpina speciosa, 36
Alsophila australis, 36
Aralia papyrifera, 36
Araucaria sp., 37
Arecastrum romanzoffianum, 37
Aspidistra elatior, 39
Aucuba japonica, 39

Bambusaceae, 39
Bauhinia sp., 42
Beloperone guttata, 42
Bougainvillea sp., 42
Bromeliaceae, 42
Brunfelsia calycina, 44
Butia capitata, 44

Cactaceae, 44
Caladium bicolor, 45
Callistemon citrinus, 46
Canna indica, 46
Carica papaya, 47
Carissa grandiflora, 47
Casurina equisetifolia, 47
Catalpa speciosa, 48
Ceratostigma plumbaginoides, 48
Chamaerops humilis, 48
Chlorophytum comosum, 48
Cinnamomum camphora, 48
Citrus sp., 49
Codiaeum variegatum, 50
Coleus blumei, 50
Commelinaceae, 50
Cortaderia sellowiana, 52
Cycas revoluta, 53
Cynara scolymus, 53

Cyperus sp., 53
Cyrtomium falcatum, 54

Dioon edule, 55
Dioscorea sp., 55

Eriobotrya japonica, 56
Erythrina crista-galli, 56
Eucalyptus sp., 56
Euphorbia pulcherrima, 57

Fatsia japonica, 58
Ficus sp., 58
Firmiana simplex, 59

Gardenia jasminoides, 59
Gerbera jamesoni, 59
Graptopetalum paraguayense, 60

Hedera helix, 60
Hedychium coronarium, 60
Heliconia sp., 61
Hibiscus rosa-sinensis, 61
Hippeastrum striatum, 62
Hymenocallis sp., 62

Impatiens sultani, 64

Jacobinia carea, 65

Koelreuteria bipinnata, 65

Lagerstroemia indica, 65
Lantana camara, 66
Liriope muscari, 66
Livistona chinensis, 67

Marsilea sp., 67
Melia azedarach, 67
Monstera deliciosa, 68
Musa sp., 68

Nandina domestica, 69
Nephrolepis exaltata, 69
Nerium oleander, 70
Nymphaea sp., 70

Onoclea sensibilis, 70
Ophiopogon japonicus, 70
Orchidiaceae, 70
Osmunda sp., 71

Parkinsonia aculeata, 73
Passiflora sp., 73
Persera americana, 74
Philodendron selloum, 74
Phoenix sp., 75
Phormium sp., 75
Plumeria sp., 76
Pothos scandens, 76
Punica granatum, 77

Raphiolepis indica, 78
Raphis excelsa, 79
Rhoeo discolor, 79

Sabal sp., 79
Salix sp., 80
Stenotaphrum secundatum, 80
Strelitzia sp., 80
Syngonium podophyllum, 81

Tabernamontana divaricata (grandiflora), 81
Trachelospermum jasminoides, 81
Trachycarpus fortunei, 82

Vitex agnus-castus, 82

Washingtonia sp., 82

Yucca aloifolia, 83

Zantedeschia sp., 83

Index, 84

Index to Botanical Names, Index to Common Names

of special interest...

Quick Coverings for Winter, 18

The Hardy, the Half-Hardy, and the Tender, 21

Tips on Garden Pools, 31

Leaf Textures, 41

All About Elephant Ears, 51

Variegation: Shades of a Another Color, 63

Palms, 72

Plants for Shaded Areas, 77

Climate Data for Southern Cities

	Last Spring Freeze	First Fall Freeze	Frost-Free Days	Record January Low (°F)	Minimum Hours of Chilling	Inches of Rain
Alabama						
Birmingham	Mar. 19	Nov. 14	241	1	1,000	53
Huntsville	Apr. 1	Nov. 8	221	−9	1,100	50
Mobile	Feb. 17	Dec. 12	298	14	500	67
Montgomery	Feb. 27	Dec. 3	279	5	700	51
Arkansas						
Little Rock	Mar. 16	Nov. 15	244	−4	1,000	49
Florida						
Jacksonville	Feb. 6	Dec. 16	313	2	400	53
Orlando	Jan. 31	Dec. 17	319	24	300	51
Tampa	Jan. 10	Dec. 26	349	23	200	51
Georgia						
Atlanta	Mar. 20	Nov. 19	244	−3	800	49
Macon	Mar. 14	Nov. 7	240	3	700	44
Savannah	Feb. 21	Dec. 9	291	9	500	48
Kentucky						
Lexington	Apr. 13	Oct. 28	198	−15	1,400	43
Louisville	Apr. 1	Nov. 7	220	−20	1,400	41
Louisiana						
Baton Rouge	Feb. 28	Nov. 30	275	10	500	55
New Orleans	Feb. 13	Dec. 9	300	14	400	64
Maryland						
Baltimore	Mar. 26	Nov. 19	238	−7	1,400	43
Mississippi						
Jackson	Mar. 10	Nov. 13	248	7	700	50
North Carolina						
Charlotte	Mar. 21	Nov. 15	239	4	900	43
Greensboro	Mar. 24	Nov. 16	237	0	1,100	43
Oklahoma						
Oklahoma City	Mar. 28	Nov. 7	223	0	1,200	32
Tulsa	Mar. 31	Nov. 2	216	−2	1,300	38
South Carolina						
Charleston	Feb. 19	Dec. 10	294	11	600	49
Columbia	Mar. 14	Nov. 21	252	5	700	47
Tennessee						
Knoxville	Mar. 31	Nov. 6	220	−16	1,100	45
Memphis	Mar. 20	Nov. 12	237	−8	1,000	49
Nashville	Mar. 28	Nov. 7	224	−6	1,100	47
Texas						
Austin	Mar. 15	Nov. 20	244	12	700	33
Dallas-Ft. Worth	Mar. 18	Nov. 17	244	5	1,000	33
Houston	Feb. 10	Dec. 8	301	19	600	44
San Antonio	Feb. 24	Dec. 3	282	0	600	26
Virginia						
Norfolk	Apr. 4	Nov. 9	219	10	1,100	44
Richmond	Apr. 20	Oct. 18	181	−12	1,200	44

A Look at the Tropics and the Gulf Coast

What Makes a Tropical Place Tropical?

To many of us, the word "tropics" conjures up visions of the hot, wet, impenetrable, disease-ridden jungles we've seen in the movies. In fact, the tropics are much more pleasant, interesting, and varied places than this. In the next few pages I want to present a more accurate view of the tropics. As you will quickly discover, the places called "tropical" are not identical or even very much alike: tropical areas comprise a very diverse group of plant communities around the equator.

I'll describe briefly some of the more important communities so you can see where many of our plants come from and the unique conditions under which they grow in nature. From this introduction to the tropics and their flora you can begin to see how to successfully grow these plants along the Gulf Coast and how to resolve certain seasonal problems that occur here.

Where are the Tropics?

The subtropical and tropical zones begin in those areas close enough to the equator to be without frost. In the Northern Hemisphere this begins at about 24 degrees north latitude, (near Tampico, Mex.) and extends south. The lower half of Florida is marginal: it gets infrequent frosts (less than every two years) but that is still enough to cause some problems in inland areas.

The zone continues through much of coastal Mexico to Central and South America and the equator. A comparable zone develops south of the equator, so that much of South America falls into the tropical zone. Tropical zones develop in a similar way in equatorial regions of Africa, India, Southeast Asia, and the South Pacific.

Not all of the areas near the equator are what one might call tropical. For a region to be tropical it must be warm and wet all year. Many areas in the near-equatorial regions are neither warm nor wet. Vast areas have little or no rain—the Atacama Desert of South America and the Sahara of Africa, for example. Many regions get only limited seasonal rain: the deserts and grasslands of Mexico, India, and East Africa. And some areas are at too high an altitude to qualify; when the altitude goes up, it gets cooler, even at the equator. Snow falls atop such equatorial mountains as Kilimanjaro in Africa and Chimborazo in South America. So, many regions of Africa, Asia, Mexico, and Central and South America are simply too high or dry to be tropical.

When you remove all of the places that should be tropical but aren't, you're left with the truly tropical and near-tropical areas. These include parts of southern Mexico, most of Central America, Amazonian South America, a relatively narrow region in Africa, much of Southeast Asia, all of the South Pacific, and Eastern Australia.

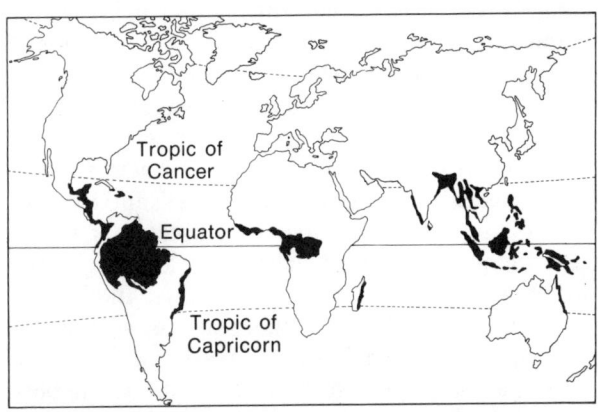

Distribution of the wet tropics (indicated in black).

What are the Tropics Like?

In parts of each of these areas the famous tropical rain forest occurs. These rain forests get lots of water year-round. Rainfall varies from 80 to 350 inches a year. This tremendous rainfall also produces year-round high humidity. Temperatures are uniformly quite warm, usually ranging from 60° to 90° throughout the year. And since it is so moist and warm, plants grow very well.

The forest is composed of three layers of trees: tall, taller, and very tall. The trees crowd out nearly all the ground vegetation except at forest clearings, along roads or in places where a tree has fallen. These three layers of trees block nearly all of the light from the ground level. Any small forest plant living there must be able to tolerate low levels of light for long periods if it is going to survive. Otherwise, nearly all the growth is in the tree tops, where vines have climbed and epiphytes like bromeliads, orchids, cacti, ferns, and peperomias are found.

Unlike the rich soils of our northern forests, tropical soils are very poor nutritionally. There are three reasons for this: First, it rains all the time so that many available nutrients are washed away without ever being used by the plants. Another reason is that all of the rain and warmth allow microbial activity to develop very quickly—there is no chance for a nice humus layer to develop because any leaves that fall are immediately attacked by the microbes. The last reason that tropical soils are poor should now be obvious: there is tremendous competition by all the plants for any nutrients that do become available.

A consequence of all this is that tropical plants tend to grow in very poor soil, so long as it is warm and damp. But there is a surprising contradiction: they can also withstand high levels of fertilization! These plants must compete aggressively for light and nutrients. If either becomes available because a tree falls or a road is cut, the plants will grow at a tremendous rate, trying to grab all of the nutrients and light before a competitor does. Given the opportunity, they are able to take advantage of food and light resources in a spectacular way.

The inside of a mature rain forest is reminiscent of a cathedral. The trees are tall spires, and there is little or no brush on the ground because it is too dark for plants to grow. You must look high into the trees to see any leaves or branches. In all, it is quite eerie, knowing that thousands of plants are growing on the branches of the trees towering over your head while you stand in the dark at the bottom of the forest.

When you come to a river's edge, a roadside or a place where a tree has fallen, the story is quite different. In these places the jungle is thick because all the plants are fighting for a place in the sun. Here is where most of the movies, and the stereotype of a dense jungle, are made.

A typical tropical rain forest. The plants here are in vigorous competition for nutrients and sunlight, which is why many tropical plants will grow in poor soils and yet respond to high fertilization.

Some of our most popular tropical house-plants come from the lowland tropical rain forest. The popular rubber plant and schefflera form huge trees, while the viny pothos and split-leaf philodendron grow up forest trees in search of light. Bananas and papayas grow at the forest's edge, while tree ferns, diffenbachias, dracaenas, and young palms grow in the dimly lit understory of the forest. In the tree branches bromeliads, peperomias, orchids, and many ferns are commonly found.

Some Variations on a Tropical Theme

Besides the "typical" tropical situation there are several other environments in near-equatorial regions that qualify as true tropical plant communities or are often thought of as tropical plant communities because so many "tropical" plants are native to them. Three of the most interesting of these communities are included here.

The Montane Rain Forest

When you begin to drive into the mountains above a tropical rain forest, you will find the air becomes cooler the higher you go. The montane rain forest is found on the lower slopes of these mountains, up to 4,000 feet. Here the air is cooler (70°-80°F) and it still rains year-round. In this forest the trees are shorter and more epiphytes and other plants are found.

Elements of this forest are found in Mexico, Central America, South America, Southeast Asia, and Africa. It is in this zone that coffee and many citrus trees are commonly grown, and most people live here rather than in the lowlands because of the amicable climate. Many of our most popular tropical plants are found here—begonias, crotons, and hibiscus, to name a few.

The Cloud Forest

Above the montane rain forest one occasionally finds an area where very cold air from the mountain top mixes with the warm, moist air from the tropical lowlands to create a cloudy, misty, wet, cold forest, sometimes called a cloud forest. The trees are quite short and are thickly covered with ferns, mosses, orchids, philodendrons, peperomias, bromeliads, etc. This forest stays barely above freezing during the cool season and is never very warm even in the "summer." The continued cold, wet climate is great for plants but it's not a very nice place to live.

Elements of this rather restricted type of forest are found in the high mountains of Mexico, South America, Africa, and the Himalayas. While the plants in this forest are in a sense tropical plants, they are adapted to constantly cool, wet conditions and will not adapt to our hot summers. Some extremely beautiful orchids and ferns grow in these areas, but they aren't adaptable to our Gulf Coast.

A montane rain forest. Many of our most popular tropical plants come from this kind of tropical environment.

The Tropical Deciduous Forest

Many equatorial areas remain warm throughout the year, get vast amounts of rain for most of the year but have a dry season of varying severity also. The forests are called tropical deciduous forests because the trees there drop their leaves in response to the dryness, not in response to the cold. All of the plants from these areas must be prepared for this dry season. Some go dormant by losing their leaves; still others quit growing but retain their leaves; still others die back to a tuber, bulb or fleshy root.

Of the three forests described, this is the most widespread, covering vast areas of Africa, Asia and limited parts of American tropical areas. Plants from this forest frequently do well in our

A typical cloud forest in a tropical region. Temperatures here can get as low as 40°, and the air is always very moist. Such forests are homes for many bromeliads, ferns, and orchids.

Tropical Climate Forests 3

area because their dormant phase coincides with our cold period. The only problem is that some of these plants cannot withstand an excess of water while dormant, causing them to rot during our winters. Typical of these plants are the famous frangipani, certain nephrytis, the elephant's foot plant, and some rhizomatous begonias.

Confusing Non-Tropical Places

By now you should understand what "tropical" means. Just to make things difficult, there are also several non-tropical areas that are frequently regarded as tropical, foremost among them Japan which is often called "warm temperate." Many tropical plants have relatives in Japan such as Japanese aralia and bamboo, and several frost-tolerant types of both are native there. Most of Japan is warm, temperate, and maritime, yet much of it receives frost each winter and snow abounds in the more northerly islands. Were it not for the closeness of the sea, Japan would be even cooler than it is—the sea moderates Japan's climate immensely.

Much of the Chinese mainland is also warm temperate. Plants from much of China need a

A tropical deciduous forest. Like tropical rain forests, these deciduous forests get vast amounts of rain; but unlike them, they also have a dry season. To prepare for this dryness, many trees and plants in this kind of tropical area lose their leaves or die back to the ground.

decided winter dormancy to flower properly (Chinese azalias and cymbidium orchids, for example).

The same is true of much of New Zealand. Only the northernmost coast of New Zealand is frost-free year-round, yet the very tropical-looking frost-tolerant New Zealand flax grows in many areas of that country.

Vast numbers of our favorite exotic plants hail from these non-tropical areas. Knowing where they come from helps us understand how to grow them and why certain of the warm temperate plants don't like our summer but do like our fall, winter, and spring.

A Look at the Gulf Coast

People around the United States envision the Gulf Coast as a very tropical area. When you compare our mild, nearly frost-free winters with those in Buffalo, New York, it's easy to see how they arrive at this conclusion. On the other hand, after weeks of dismal January weather those of us along the Gulf begin to feel we are entering a new Ice Age. Of course, neither view is really correct. We

The "warm temperate" forest. This type of plant habitat is common to Japan, parts of China, and New Zealand. Though these areas are not tropical at all, many exotic plants are native to them.

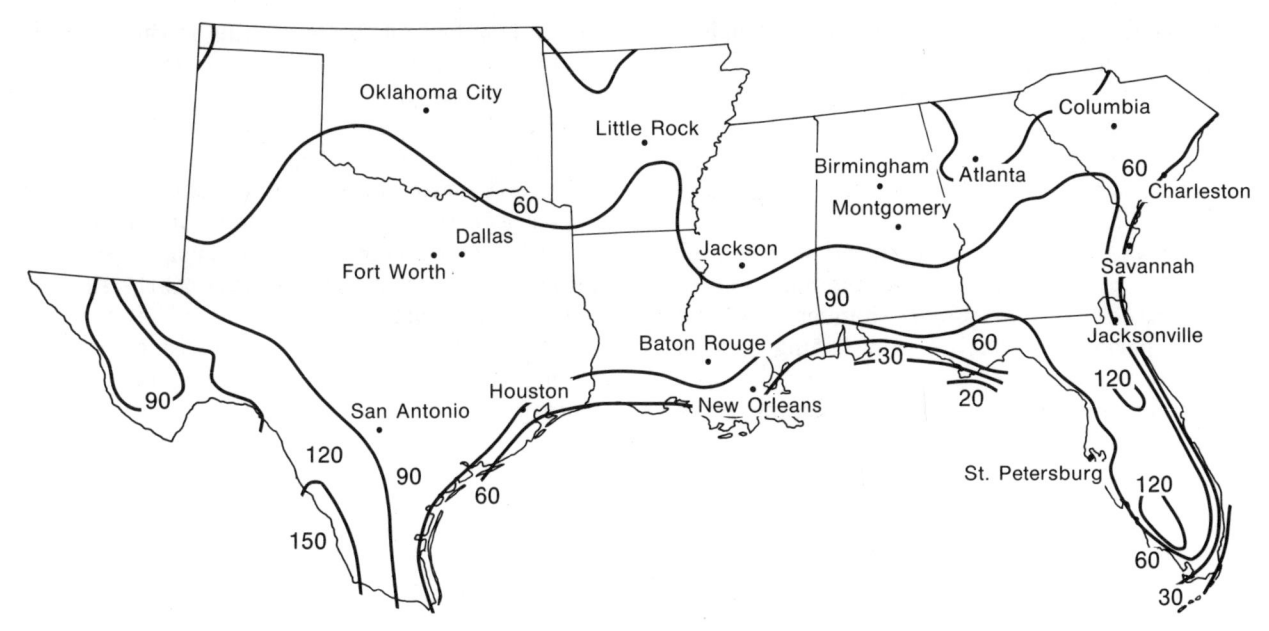

Heat in the lower South: Mean annual number of days that temperatures are 90°F or higher.

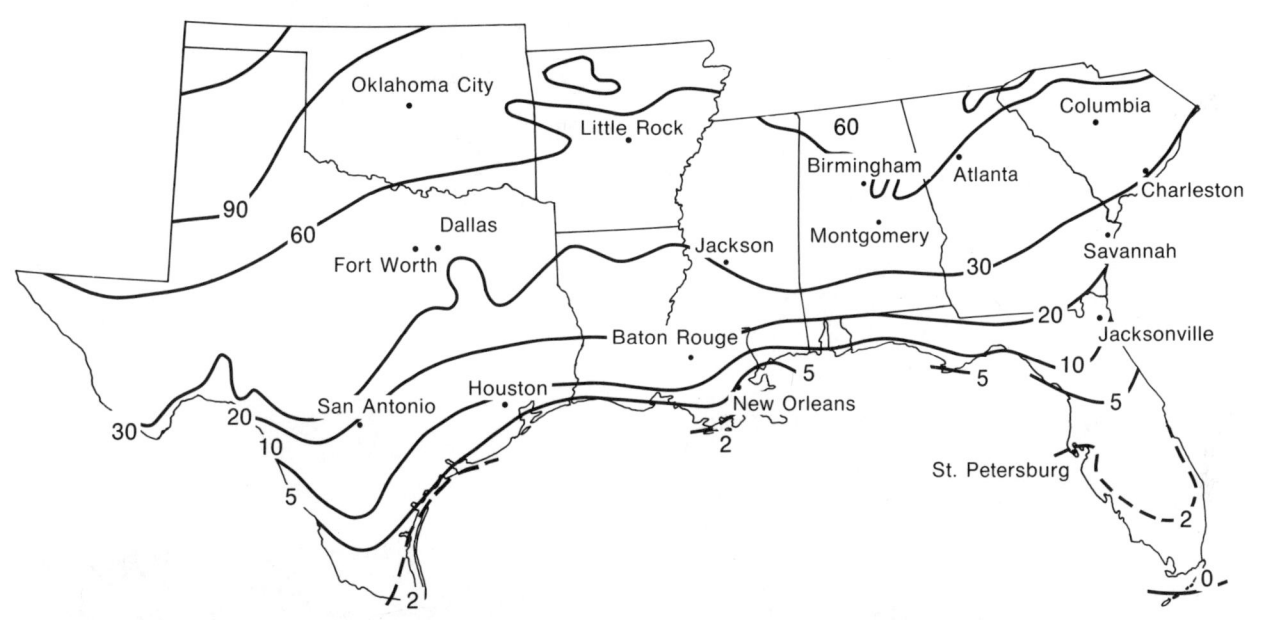

Freezes in the lower South: Mean annual number of days that temperatures are 32°F or lower.

have our own distinctive weather here and at various times it resembles the seasons in other places throughout the world.

Now let's look at how our Gulf Coast weather resembles and contrasts with the weather of some of the tropical areas just discussed.

How Gulf Coast Seasons Resemble Tropical Seasons

The weather along the Gulf Coast has three distinct phases. Summer is the most prominent, lasting at least five months from mid-May to mid-October. Our summers are very warm and last longer than the summers to the north, but there are fewer *very* hot days than you might expect. This is indicated by the temperature map (above).

Our rainfall in the summer comes in short quick showers, and throughout our region rainfall is generally abundant all year. This is illustrated in the rainfall map (top, page 6). And, of course, we have continuously high humidity, usually over 60 percent, along the Gulf Coast (see the humidity map, bottom of page 6).

In the summer season the Gulf Coast has all the characteristics of a Turkish bath. It also strongly

The Gulf Coast 5

resembles the conditions in a true lowland tropical rain forest. During our summer most tropical garden plants grow profusely. Bamboos will grow 30-foot shoots in a few weeks; bananas grow 6- to 8-foot leaves weekly; the philodendrons completely take over, while we gardeners hide in our air-conditioned homes.

Spring and fall comprise a collective season of about four months. Rainfall remains high, and in addition to the short but intense thunderstorms we also get periods of soaking rain lasting several days. Day temperatures can reach into the upper 80s but nights are refreshingly cool, ranging in the middle 50s. For me, at least, this is the most enjoyable time. This season resembles the conditions of the montane rain forest, and the cooler-growing tropicals have a field day while the hot-growing tropicals just about quit growing.

Our last season, and the most dismal, is winter. Days are in the 50s to 60s; nights in the low 40s with lots of slow rain and an occasional frost. The tropical cloud forests are like this nearly all year. Any of the cool-growing tropical and warm temperate plants that have survived our savage summer feel right at home during our normal winter.

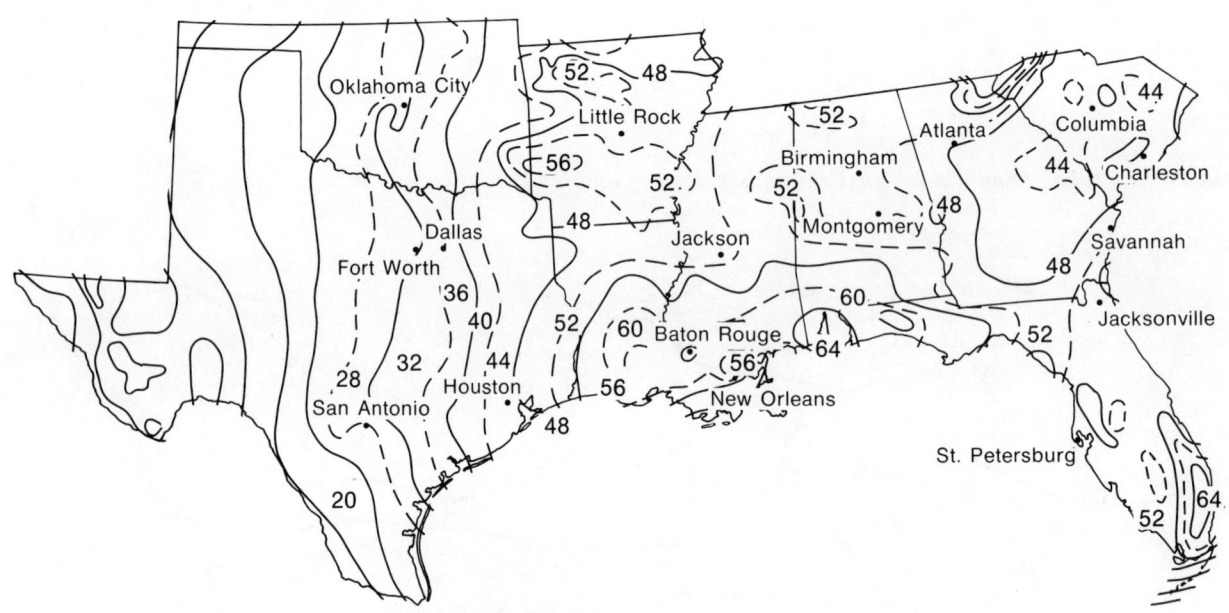

Normal yearly rainfall (inches) in the lower South.

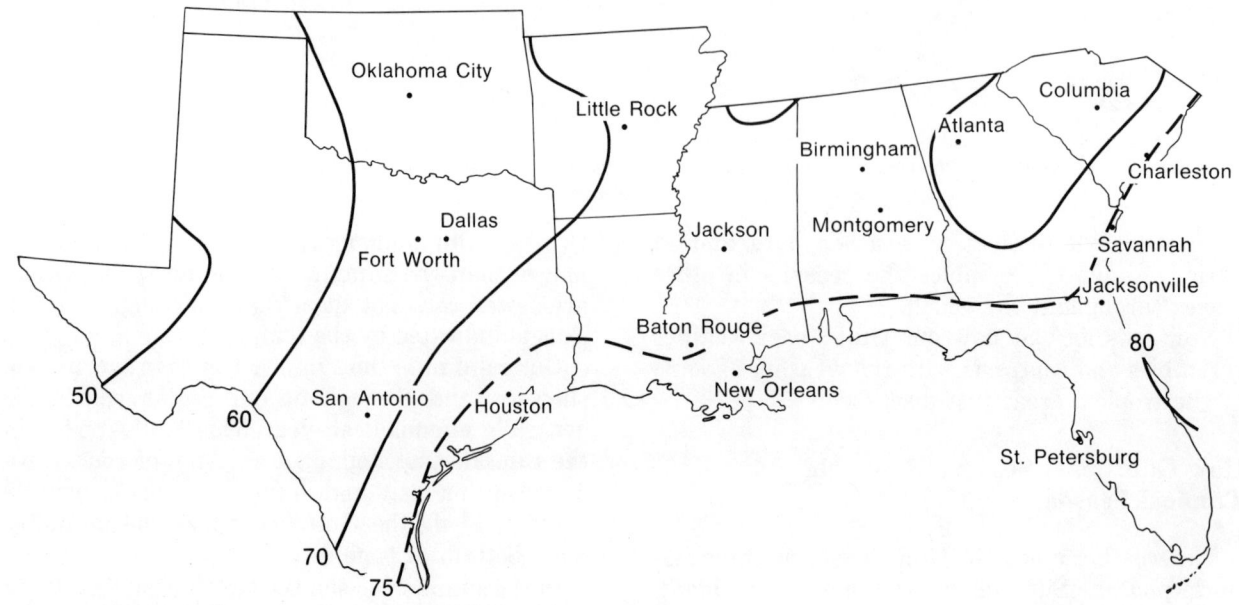

Mean annual relative humidity (percent) in the lower South.

6   The Gulf Coast Climate

Seasonal Variations That Can Cause Problems

Each of our seasons creates conditions suitable to plants from one place but detrimental to plants from another. In addition to these overall seasonal peculiarities, the Gulf Coast has an additional set of less predictable variables that can cause problems to the unprepared gardener.

The great problem to tropical gardening in our area is the unpredictability of the weather. If you study the weather records for the area, you'll discover that our region is characterized by hot summers and moderate winters. Rainfall is generally uniform throughout the year. Frost is present but usually occurs only 2 to 15 times a year, while drought periods usually don't last for more than a couple of weeks. Realizing all of this, you'd think you could grow any tropical you wish throughout the year, perhaps with some minor winter protection. If only the weather would read the record books, we could rest easy! As it turns out, weather along the Gulf Coast is characterized by occasional deviations from the norms.

Droughts

Our weather goes on binges. Droughts of six to eight weeks duration can strike at *any* time. These always seem to be followed by periods of extraordinary rain, on the order of 2 inches a day for weeks. During the drought period the entire garden dries up. Great cracks form in the soil, all the trees and plants wilt, watering seems to be of no avail because the next day more water is needed. Then along comes the rain: everything gets soggy, the roots rot, the leaves die. It stays so cloudy for so long that the plants sunburn when the sun finally comes out.

Hard Freezes

Winters are a frustration all their own. Besides occasional droughts and the more typical wet periods, we have unpredictable cold spells to contend with. Many winters may pass with one or a few brief frosts that never drop below 28°F. The map of mean numbers of days below 32°F (see page 6) gives our typical wintertime frost picture. About one year in ten a severe freeze hits; temperatures drop to the teens, the wind blows hard, everything freezes. These freezes are devastating when followed by a long wet period that allows all the frost-damaged plants to rot.

It's easy to water a dry plant; it's relatively easy to protect a plant from too much rain; but handling a severe freeze requires foresight and planning for an event that may not come for years.

Frost Duration. Frost in the South differs significantly from frost in areas further north. The difference is in duration. In northern areas like Denver, Kansas City or St. Louis, a temperature of 25°F may last for 8 to 10 hours or on occasion, for several days. Meanwhile a freeze of 25°F in Houston, Mobile or Tallahassee normally lasts only an hour or two and frequently for only a few minutes before the temperature begins to rise again.

Because most southern freezes are of short duration, we can grow many tropical plants which are not otherwise adapted to our winters. A freeze of long duration will kill a banana to the ground and below, causing death to the plant. Short, hard freezes, by contrast, may kill the leaves, but the thick stem will not be hurt because its thickness acts as insulation, which delays the cooling. In short freezes the stem will never even get close to freezing; the stem and roots remain protected, warm, and ready to grow as soon as all chance of frost is gone.

Heat Islands. Many gardeners have found that some of the more tender plants can be grown in the city but not in the suburbs. This is because cities create heat islands. A heat island is a "bubble" of warm air that sits over nearly all large cities, causing city temperatures to be warmer than the surrounding areas. The source of this heat is obvious: cars, trucks, industry, houses, etc.—they all give off heat. In large cities so much heat is lost to the air that the outside actually warms a little.

In areas like our coastal South, enough heat is produced to keep winter night temperatures 5° to 8°F warmer than the surrounding countryside. We seldom have a freeze that goes below 25°, and in areas with heat islands, the plants in the middle of town would not freeze due to the extra heat provided by all the houses, cars and industry.

Big cities have larger heat islands than smaller cities. This makes sense since big cities have more industry, etc. giving off heat. But don't depend upon heat islands to protect your tender plants on *windy*, cold nights. A heavy wind on a cold night will blow much of the heat away. When this happens, the central part of the city will be much cooler because the protective heat layer is blown away.

Why We Have These Peculiar Weather Problems

The problem is this: the Gulf Coast is to the southeast of the rest of the continent. During good weather, winds prevail out of the southeast to bring warm moist air ("tropical conditions") in off

Weather Extremes 7

Though we do have freezes in the South, they are rather brief, especially along the Gulf Coast. It is this short duration of low temperatures that, more than any other factor, allows us to grow so many tropical plants outdoors.

the very warm Gulf of Mexico. The only storms we get from the Gulf are hurricanes. These are infrequent but on occasion devastating. Our major weather comes from the northwest. Arctic fronts sweep down all winter, and since they do not pass over water, they tend to be very harsh. Particularly strong ones will push out all of the warm air that we normally have and bring the occasional very cold weather. At other times they will stall out and cause two weeks of rain, or a blocking high-pressure system will not allow any to pass and we get a big drought.

What Does All This Mean?

By looking at tropical areas for a moment and comparing these areas to our Gulf Coast we can begin to see what accommodations we can make to grow some of our favorite tropical plants. To successfully develop a tropical garden, you must care for it as you care for any garden—with interest and foresight. You must expect the unusual and the unpredicted. So long as we are under the tropical weather influence our gardens are fairly easy, but temperate and arctic weather can affect us adversely.

Even though you take precautions, you must realize that occasionally frost will kill out favorite plants and droughts will do the same. In trying to grow a tropical garden in a non-tropical area we are playing a game of roulette, and once in a while we will lose. If the southern United States were always perfect for tropical plants they would be here already and we would not need to plant them!

In the bulk of this book I'll relate these previous discussions to resolving the specific problems we will encounter as our tropical gardens develop. In addition to the tropical material, I've also included many non-tropical plants from Japan, China, New Zealand, etc. I've included any tropical or tropical-looking plants no matter what their origin. Most of these plants are typified by large leaves, fast growth, exotic flowers, and some susceptibility to cold. The plants discussed here are usually seen in tropical gardens, but I've added a few surprises when I felt they'd make a contribution to your garden.

How to Care for Your Tropical Garden

Tropical gardens, like most gardens, thrive on care and attention. Tropical gardens grow best when each specimen in the garden is provided with the conditions suited to its particular growing requirements. Yet, certain gardening practices are beneficial to all tropical plants. Rich soil, abundant moisture, proper light, and freedom from crowding will make all members of the garden happy. These general factors of successful gardening are the subject of this section.

Once you've provided a generally good situation for your plants, you'll find that providing the special requirements of your favorite tree fern, or whatever, is very easy. Most plants will thrive under the conditions discussed here; if a plant has any special requirements, the specifics will be covered later in a special section devoted to that plant (pages 33-83).

Soil Preparation

Soil conditions will dictate the success or failure of your tropical garden. In our region we have either clay soil or very sandy soil. Only a few of us have the ideal sandy loam which is essential to successful gardening. In addition to the usual need to develop a good soil, we have to cope with periodic wet and dry spells that put special demands on our garden soils.

Ideally, the garden soil should be composed of ⅓ sand, ⅓ humus and ⅓ soil. It should be spongy and dark with a slightly acid pH of 6.0-6.8. This combination will provide the necessary drainage we need during wet periods but will retain enough moisture to keep droughts from being so devastating. And though native tropical soils are poor, remember that tropical plants respond magnificently to a good soil.

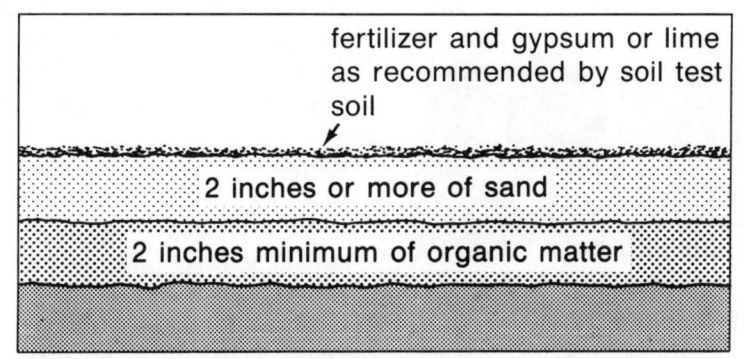

The best soil mix for your tropical garden is 2 inches of sand, 2 inches of humus (organic matter) worked into the top 2 inches or more of soil. You should also add fertilizer and gypsum (acid) or lime (alkali) as recommended by a soil test. Spread these amendments evenly on top of the soil and work them in thoroughly with a rototiller or hand tools.

Few gardeners find their soil perfect to begin with. Some item will almost certainly need to be added. If your soil is of a clay nature, sand becomes a critical addition. Sand is available from a variety of sources. Unquestionably the best is referred to as builder's sharp sand, sometimes called torpedo sand. This is the type frequently used in sand boxes and for mortar in masonry work. It is somewhat coarse or "sharp," it is well-washed, has no salts or clay in it, and is comparatively more expensive than other kinds but is definitely worthwhile.

Bank sand, though cheaper and more readily available, has a much finer particle size and some clay particles still in it—it's not nearly as good as sharp sand. If you need a great deal of sand you may want to consider bank sand because it is cheaper. Stay away from any beach sands or sand thay may contain sea salts. Traces of these salts are very difficult to wash out and their presence can ruin your garden soil.

Humus

Humus (decomposed organic matter) is something no soil seems to have enough of, and (at least here in the South) it doesn't last very long when it's added. There are a couple of reasons for this. One is our hot sultry summers, which induce abundant microbial action that completely breaks any plant matter down. The other reason is that much of our soil has been brought in by wind and water, so that most of the larger soil particles have long since been removed, leaving us with a very tight clay soil. This soil absolutely requires humus to "open it up" and allow places for roots to grow and air to permeate. Air, especially oxygen, is critical to root growth, and clay soils tend to exclude oxygen when they get wet, but humus in the soil allows good aeration.

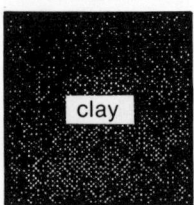

clay	silt	sand
very few air spaces	small air spaces	large air spaces

Air-holding capacity of sand, silt, and clay soils.

In areas with very sandy soil, previous water activity has brought all the sand of a given particle size together and removed all smaller or larger particles and all the humus. Again we must add humus, this time to enhance the soil's water-retention capacity. In sandy soils the roots get so much drainage they dry out. Humus alleviates this effect and provides a source of nutrition to the plant.

There are a variety of imaginative sources for humus, including peat moss, rice hulls, leaves, pine needles, compost, etc. Each has its virtues and drawbacks. Peat moss is expensive because it is shipped in from limited deposits up north. Also, it is very poor in nutrients, but it is acid and will help if you have an alkaline soil. Don't confuse *peat moss* with peat. Peat moss is a very light, brown milled moss that looks somewhat like coffee. Peat, the bog soil, is a heavy black mud-like soil. Peat moss is sold by the cubic foot; peat, is sold by the 50-lb. bag. Both help the soil in various ways, but peat moss is much more effective in "opening" the soil.

Rice hulls can be gathered from any rice mill. They are a very workable form of humus, are cheaper than peat moss, and add more nutrients to the soil. They are also frequently harder to locate, but they're worth the effort. Leaves and pine needles can both be spread around the garden. If you have an acidity problem, pine needles are especially useful since they are very acid. Otherwise, oak or any other leaves are good and quite cheap. In the fall your neighbors will just give them to you. Think of these gifts as vegetable gold, not as your neighbor's refuse.

Compost. This is an excellent source of humus for the garden. Composting can be as simple or as complex as you want to make it. I prefer to keep it simple.

Compost bins are easily made out of welded wire or old boards. Each layer of the pile should be 4 to 6 inches thick, overlain with 2 inches of soil. Continue the process until the pile is about 4 feet tall. Add some fertilizer once in a while and let it set. The pile will heat up then cool off and shrink; at that point it is ready for use. For more on compost, see Bill Adams's *Vegetable Growing for Southern Gardens*, Pacesetter Press, Houston, Tx.

Water

Knowing how to water is another key to a successful garden. Tropicals like to be kept evenly damp; too wet and they rot, too dry and they stunt. Ideally, your soil should be porous enough to allow excess water to drain off; yet it should contain enough humus to hold supplemental water you may need to add during dry periods.

If your garden has gone five to seven days without measurable rain, it will probably be quite dry since these plants all have very high water requirements. When it's necessary to water, do a good job. Don't swish the nozzle aimlessly about and forget it. Each section of your garden will want about 1 inch of water a week. If you use sprinklers, check their output by placing a can about midway between the sprinkler head and the spray edge. When an inch of water collects in the can, move the sprinkler to another spot. Soil irrigation by flooding channels at the edge of the garden works well, but you'll still have to put some water on the beds themselves or local dry spots will develop which may be detrimental to any small, shallow rooted plants in the center of the bed.

Fertilizer

Since nearly all tropicals are voracious feeders, provide consistently high levels of fertilization throughout the growing season so they can perform well. Any high analysis fertilizer (30-10-10 or 20-20-20) can be used. Sprinkle it in each bed monthly from April to September and water it in. Alternative sources of fertilizer include any humus or compost which can be spread over the soil (but not on top of the plants) several times during the growing season. Mulches of hay and leaves can be built up also (in addition to keeping weeds out and moisture in, these add nutrients too).

It is important to fertilize regularly in lesser amounts rather than less frequently in larger amounts. Most of these plants grow as they receive the nutrients, but they do not store them. If you fertilize infrequently, the plants will start and stop growing in phase with your feeding schedule, causing the garden to develop a rather peculiar pattern of lush and starved growth on each plant.

With such a heavy feeding schedule, it will be necessary to keep the garden well-watered, weed-free, and *roomy*—in a bed of mixed tropicals one or a few will nearly always try to take over and crowd out their neighbors.

Soil pH

Soil pH refers to the soil's acidity or alkalinity. The pH is measured on a scale of 0 to 14, with 7 being neutral, below 7 being acid, above 7 alkaline. Generally, damp forest soils are acid and dry desert soils are alkaline. However, this is not always true, so you must test the soil or have someone else test it with a soil test kit. You can send a sample to your local agricultural Extension agent's office, where they will analyze it for a small fee. Many garden shops will analyze it also. Once you know what your garden soil has and lacks, you will be ahead on how to balance it out for a successful tropical garden.

Ideally, the garden soil should be about 6.0 to 6.8, or slightly acid. Alkaline soils (pH 7.5-8.5) are common. If yours is alkaline, add sulfur to it or mulch with pine needles, peat moss or oak leaves. If your soil is extremely acid (5.0 or less), add lime or similar materials to bring the soil back to the 6.0-6.8 range.

Preparing the Beds

Now that you know what your garden needs, you must put it together. You should place your beds in a sunny to partially sunny location getting at least 4 hours of sun per day. It is true that many tropicals like shade, but it's better to start with lots of sun and create shady areas beneath the taller sun-loving plants than to be restricted to only the shade-loving plants, which are shorter and tend to be less colorful.

Remove any groundcover or grass from your garden bed and put it into your compost pile. If your soil is sandy, add humus; if it's clay, add humus and sand. Since you will have completed the soil test by now, you'll know whether you must add any lime or sulfur to correct the pH.

Dig or till all the ingredients together. Most tropicals are shallow-rooted and do better in raised beds, so it isn't necessary to dig too deeply into the ground. Six inches deep will do, and if you build high beds, you may not have to dig at all. Railroad ties, boards, blocks, bricks, etc., can all be used to hold elevated beds in place. I have even built mounded beds without any sides. It is all a matter of how you have constructed your garden. As long as your soil mix is ⅓ soil, ⅓ sand, ⅓ humus the plants care little whether the bed has railroad ties around it or not. Just be sure the prepared bed is 6 to 8 inches high or deep.

Spacing

Positioning your plants is important since so many of the tropicals get very large. Ideally, each plant of the larger sort should be kept on a 6-foot center, i.e., 6 feet from its nearest neighbors. Some of the smaller ones will survive on 3-foot centers, but even these will crowd out in a year or two. If you feel that putting small tropicals 6 feet apart will took too sparse, try this approach: plant your main tropical plants, those you know will not be moved, on a 6 foot center and place other similar or different satellite filler plants in between. As everything grows, remove the satellites to make room for the developing main plants.

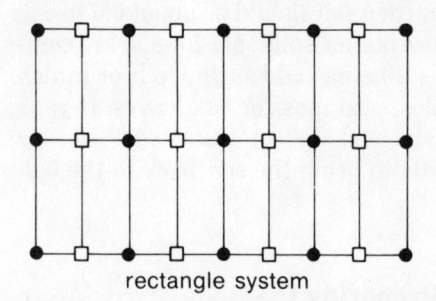

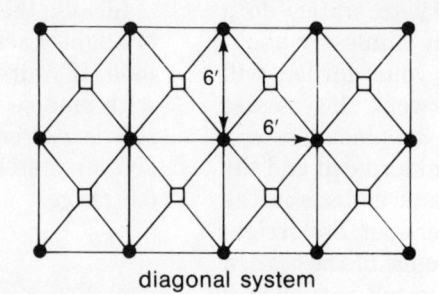

Using filler plants: place your larger-growing tropicals at least 6 feet apart. When the plants are very young, this may make the garden look sparse, but you can place temporary filler plants (□) in between until the larger plants (●) mature.

Pests

Insects

Bugs aren't much of a problem with the tropicals listed in this book. One never sees a banana tree with bites out of the leaves, and only a mad insect would try to munch on a bamboo. Leaf rollers occasionally attack cannas and the new growth of various shrubs. Red spiders sometimes build up in late summer when it's hot and dry. Mealy bugs may attack a ricepaper plant or two, but really, tropicals are seldom bothered by any severe insect problems.

As a precaution, spray a general-purpose insecticide monthly each summer. I prefer the systemic-type insecticides, which are especially effective against mealy bugs, white fly, aphids and the like. If you are worried about spraying too much, you can wait for an infestation to break out and spot treat it as necessary.

Our damp climate does encourage the development of snails and slugs. Both live in dark, damp holes by day and crawl about at night for dinner. There are a variety of slug and snail baits available, any of which should be broadcast in the garden periodically, but especially during the spring and after long periods of rain.

Pill bugs or sow bugs and the very similar wood lice are handled in ways similar to the snails and slugs. Several baits are available and these should be broadcast with reasonable frequency. Wood lice and pill bugs reproduce at a fantastic rate and can do considerable damage to your garden if left uncontrolled.

The big native cockroach is everywhere in our area. They are especially fond of flower buds and will do a great deal of damage if given a chance. Normal spraying around the house, compost pile, and other hiding places works well to keep them under control.

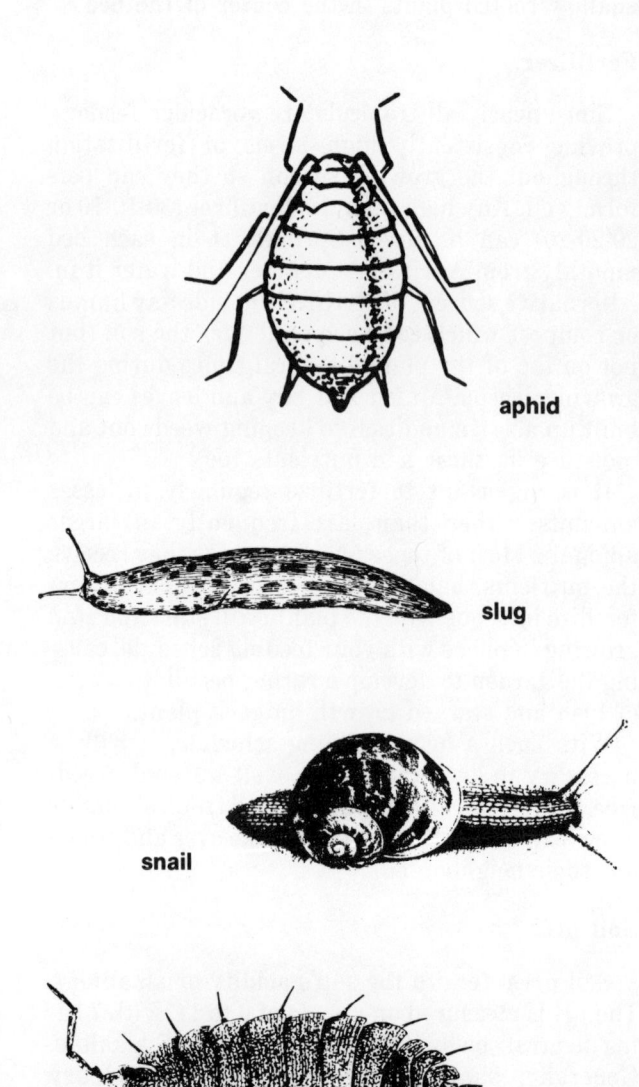

Most tropical plants are seldom attacked by pests, but when they are, the bugs shown here are likely culprits.

Diseases

Generally, tropicals seem to be disease-free. Our main problems seem to be related to rot caused by excessive rain. Soil aeration is important for keeping roots from rotting, and if you keep it aerated you'll alleviate most of your disease problems.

Occasionally one sees rust or black rot on the leaves, but each of these diseases can be treated by any of the common fungicides available. Viruses are the only difficult problem. Certain strains of tropical plants have a virus in them. This virus cannot be controlled, and if the plant appears to be suffering, it must be destroyed. Examples of viruses are the red stain seen on many amaryllis bulbs and the leaf edge and blade yellowing on some taros. Not a great deal can be done about these problems other than removal of the infected individuals.

Propagation

Propagating your plants is part of the real fun of gardening, and most tropicals are inordinately easy to propagate. In fact, you'll have a problem finding new homes for all the young plants. There are several ways to start tropicals: division, cuttings, runners, seeds, and layering.

Division

Most tropicals are propagated by division of the parent plant into several new clumps. Bananas, bamboo, cannas, cast iron plants and many others are normally propagated this way.

Plant division is very easy. All you do is dig up the plant, cut it apart, and replant it. For most plants, division is done in the spring just as the new growth begins and when new roots are forming naturally.

It is important to keep each new segment large enough. Too often, people try to get a few more divisions by making each one very small. By doing this, all you get is a large number of stunted plants that are too small to develop quickly, and you end up destroying the parent plant. It is definitely better to keep your divisions larger with several stems and healthy roots. Remember to cut the tops back on any plant you dig. By removing most of the tops you will allow the plant to grow new roots more quickly since it will not have to support the extra foliage. If you don't trim the tops you will shock the plant and slow it down unnecessarily.

While most tropicals are divided in the spring, bamboos are a notable exception. Clumping bamboos grow during our late summer, so it's best to transplant and divide them in August just as they're beginning to grow. Running bamboos may be divided in the spring or in August since they grow at both times.

Tropical plant propagation by dividing or separating.

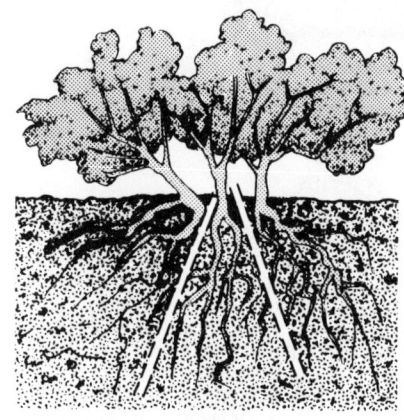

division of clumping tropicals such as bamboo, canas, and cast iron plant

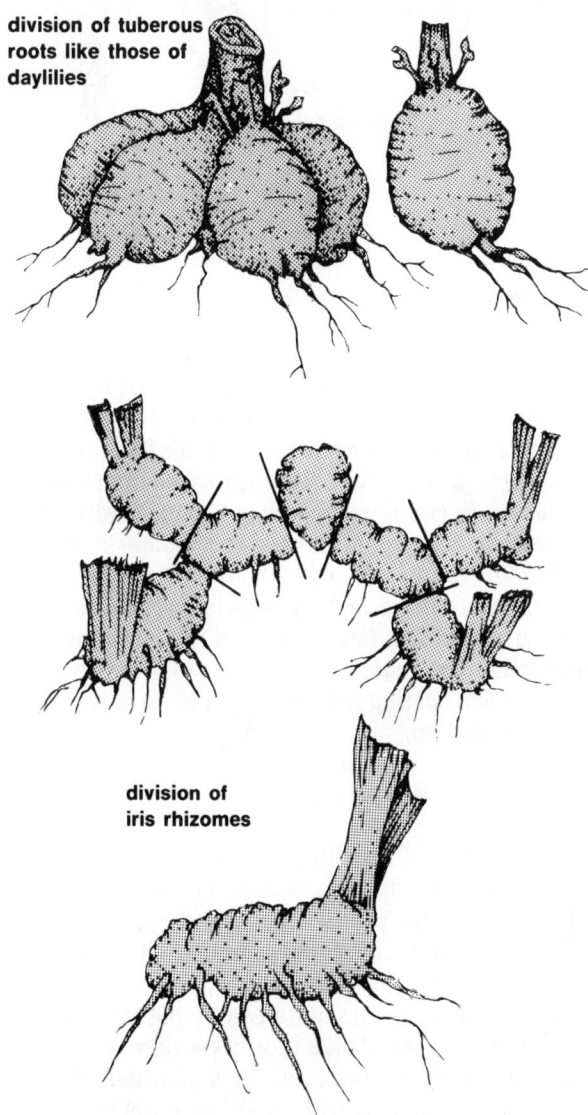

division of tuberous roots like those of daylilies

division of iris rhizomes

separation of gladiolus cormlets

division of caladium tubers

division of scales of true lilies

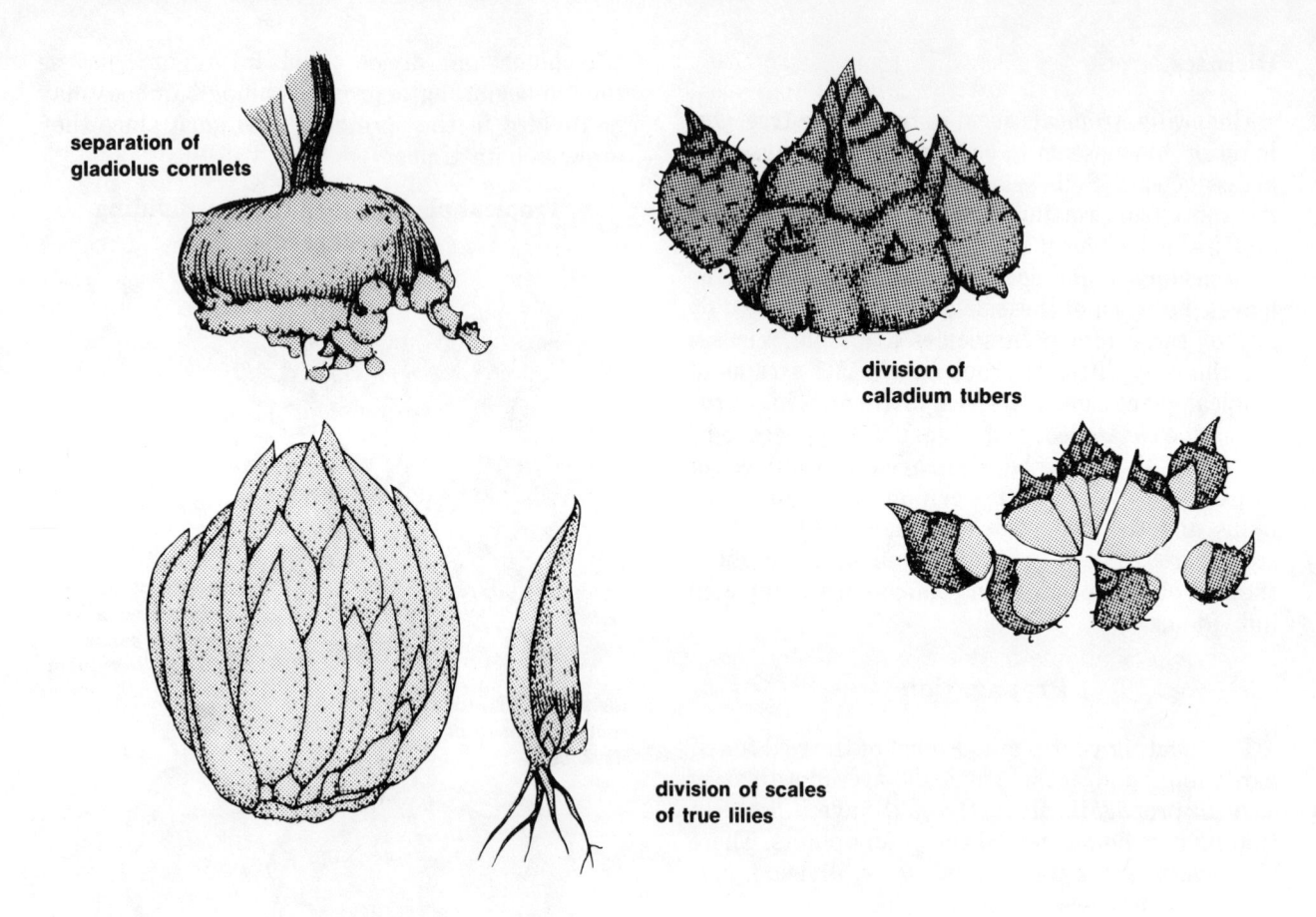

Cuttings

Many woody tropicals like hibiscus, alamanda, and bleeding heart are easily propagated by making cuttings of mature current-season growth. Each cutting should be about 8 inches long and cut just below a leaf base. Remove three-quarters of the leaves to cut down on water loss. Then dip each cutting in rooting hormone and place in damp perlite or sand. Cuttings should be placed in a damp, shady place or in a plastic bag where they won't dry out. In a few weeks you'll see new leaves, indicating that roots have formed. At this time you can pot each cutting individually and later transfer it to the garden.

Runners

Many plants form little plantlets on long runners. Airplane plants, strawberry begonias, and others are easily propagated by simply removing the small plants or runners when they are big enough to show roots at the bottom of the little plantlet. These small plants can be potted directly into damp soil or placed in a glass of water for a few days until roots form, then planted. Either way, the new plants will establish quickly.

A tropical plant cutting properly trimmed and inserted into the propagating medium.

A variation on this is found in those plants that voluntarily develop roots along their stems. Screw pines, wandering jew, dracaenas and others frequently show roots developing along their stems. These are easily removed and treated as runners, potting them directly or putting them in water to develop roots first.

Seeds

Most of the tropicals we use in our gardens are large plants propagated by division. However, some can be grown successfully from seeds. Many gardeners try their luck with papayas, amaryllis, bird of paradise, and even certain bananas. Seeds of all of these and many more tropicals are treated in essentially the same way.

Seeds should be planted in a sterilized mix made of ⅓ sand, ⅓ humus, and ⅓ soil. You can sterilize the soil in an oven or pressure cooker, or even have it chemically treated. An easier way is to purchase a package of sterilized potting mix.

Plant seeds at a soil depth of twice the width of the seed. Then water and place in a warm, shady place. When the seedlings begin to come up, they should be kept moist and given good light but not full sun. Many people use a shallow container for their seedlings and cover it with plastic. I prefer to use a deeper flower pot that holds moisture more evenly and cover only the top of the pot with plastic until the seeds germinate. At this point I remove the plastic and keep the soil in the flower pot damp.

Tropicals are frequently slow to germinate, so don't give up after two weeks. Also, some seedlings seem to be slow developing until they are of reasonable size, so watch them carefully. Usually, most tropicals will reach maturity in two to three years, but some will take longer in our area. Growing from seed is slower than other ways of propagation, but you usually end up with more plants. Sometimes seed growing is the only way to get certain items, and you do have a definite pride in plants you have sown yourself.

Layering

Layering is a special technique by which you can root cuttings without removing them from the mother plant. This is the only way to consistently propagate plants that root very slowly, such as rubber plants.

Layering is quite simple and can be done in two ways. The most common way for tropicals is a

Air Layering

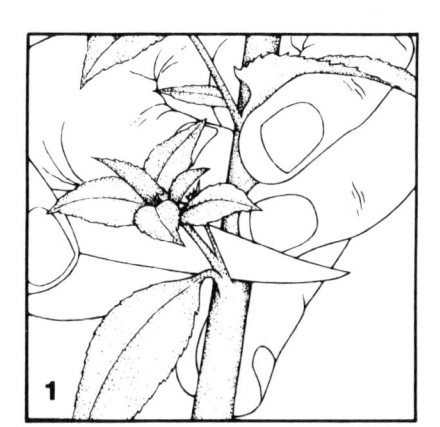

1 *Strip off leaves at axil*

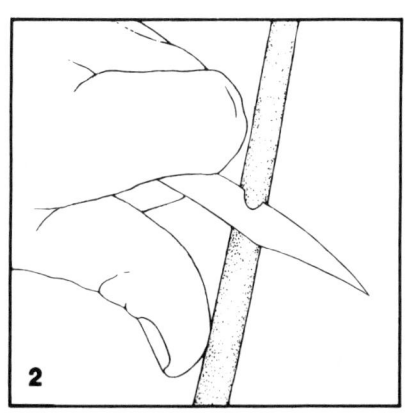

2 *Make a sloped cut to expose cambium, insert a small pebble or stick to keep the wound open, and dust wound with rooting powder.*

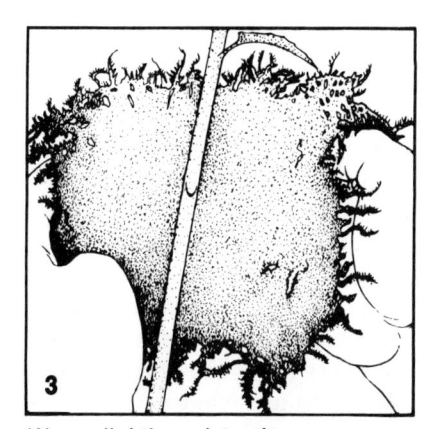

3 *Wrap slightly moist sphagnum moss around exposed surface*

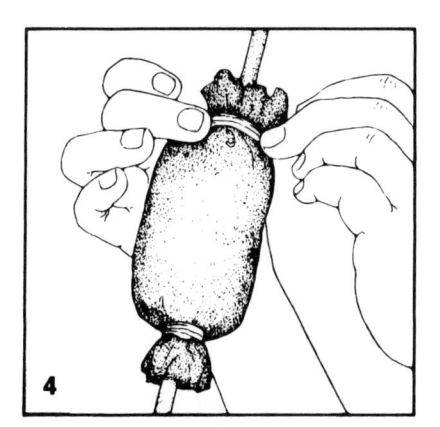

4 *Seal sphagnum moss in plastic*

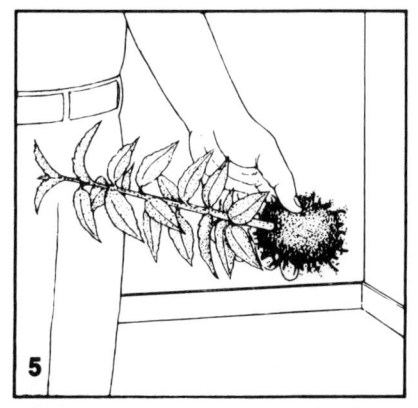

5 *Adequate roots will develop in 8 to 12 weeks; sever the shoot from the mother plant and pot in its own container.*

6

technique called *air layering*. With this method you choose a branch of a convenient length, perhaps 2 feet long, and cut a notch one-third of the way through the branch and dust the wound with rooting powder. Place a large handful of damp leaf sphagnum moss around the branch. Then wrap a piece of plastic around the moss ball to hold it in place and tie at both ends to hold the moss in the bag.

Now you wait; sometimes two weeks, sometimes eight. Eventually, a number of large white roots will form and fill the bag. Be sure to keep the moss evenly damp. Some gardeners use black plastic because they feel that light inhibits root growth.

The second way to layer is even easier. For bushes that branch profusely at ground level, you simply bend a branch down to the ground and cover it with soil. Again, it takes some time, but what's the hurry? You're only going to have to move the new plant when it is rooted. Cutting a notch in the layered branches will help them to root quicker. You should also stake the branch down to prevent it from popping up before it roots.

Special Techniques for Tropical Plant Survival

This section will show you special techniques for growing healthy tropical plants when the environment becomes adverse. Excessive heat, cold, rainfall, and drought are more of a threat to the survival of tropical plants than are insects and diseases. The problems I have repeatedly encountered always seem to relate back to extremes of the weather and its physical effect on the plants. But there are ways to alleviate the impact of weather, and these are what we'll look at next.

Cold

For many tropicals, cold is the harshest aspect of our climate. Normally we see little in the way of severe weather here, as it rarely goes below 26° F. On occasion—perhaps every few years—truly severe weather wrecks our gardens. There are a variety of ways to avoid this.

Temporary structures. A special section is devoted to this topic (page 18). In general, any cover that keeps the heat in and the wind out will suffice. If your garden is near the house, a lean-to structure which derives some of its heat and support from the house will work well. For self-supporting structures away from the house, a heating cable, light bulb or small electric heater will provide enough supplemental heat to get tender vegetation through. It's important to have a way to vent or quickly remove any structure during the daytime. Bright sun playing on the plastic will quickly create a lethal amount of heat in an enclosed space.

Mulches. Made from a variety of sources, mulches can be used to protect low vegetation. Open, spongy-textured mulches such as leaves, rice hulls, and the like can be mounded over the crowns in late fall to help protect your plants, but wait until the weather has cooled or else the mulch will stimulate new growth.

Ground-Level Branching. When you go to a nursery to choose planting stock, pick multiple-crowned rather than single-crowned plants. Multiple-crowned plants have a series of buds at or below ground level that can regenerate a lost top if frost occurs. Single-crowned plants tend to lose these ground level buds and therefore have a greater chance of not recovering from a hard freeze. Try to induce this ground-level branching on tender plants.

Special Cultivars. Plants vary in their ability to withstand cold. Keep your eyes open for individuals that are less affected by frost than others

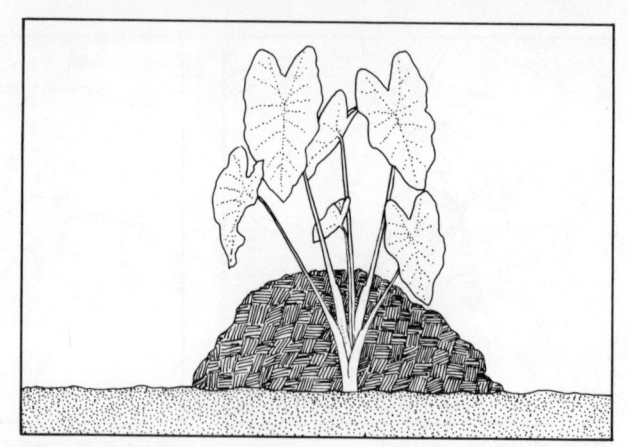

Should the leaves and stems of your plants be killed by frost, they can always regrow from the crown at the base of the plant. Protect the crown by mounding a loose mulch high over it.

Multiple-crowned plants have a series of growth buds at or below ground level and can regenerate a lost top if freeze damage occurs. Single-crowned plants tend to lose these ground level buds and thus are more likely to be completely lost to a freeze.

Helping the Plants Survive

of the same species (and check the list on pages 18-21). Also, get cuttings and divisions of locally grown plants. Plants brought in from out of state may be the same species, but they may not have the same frost hardiness.

Cuttings. On plants of uncertain hardiness, remove cuttings or suckers in the fall and treat them as houseplants until spring. This insures more plants for next year if you lose some outside. When the parent plant is fully established, you need not continue the practice, especially if the established plant is multiple-crowned. Putting a small, heated, temporary greenhouse next to the house and planting a number of cuttings in the ground inside is an easy way to bring a large variety of plants through the winter. Early the next spring, dismantle the greenhouse and transplant the cuttings back into the garden. Remember to provide water and ventilate the structure.

Protected Plantings. The east and south sides of each house are generally the more protected sides since the storms come to us from the northwest. Putting your garden on the protected side of the house is a great advantage. Enclosed entryways, covered walks, fences, garages, etc. all add to the protection.

Rain

Wet conditions can be nearly as bad as cold conditions. It's true that most tropicals thrive on water, but it can be overdone. During excessively rainy periods the ground will become so saturated that all the oxygen is used up or removed. Roots use oxygen for metabolism. It's important for them—roots can drown from lack of oxygen.

The best way to alleviate the wetness problem is to provide excellent soil drainage, and elevated beds are a good way to insure this. Sidings for raised beds may be of cedar, redwood, railroad ties, bricks, rocks, or merely mounds with sloping sides.

The soil should be very sandy with lots of humus. When working the beds, avoid walking on them. Walking on the soft, spongy bed compresses the soil and defeats the purpose of raising it. For very flat yards, drainage pipes may be a requirement. Small drainage ditches can also be dug around existing beds to help lower the water table and provide a way to irrigate during dry periods.

Cacti and other dry soil plants should be planted on a small mound of pure sand. The roots will grow through it to the soil, while the plant base will not be sitting in water when it rains. If you have a lot of dry-growing plants, consider a raised bed under the house eaves. Most of the time our rain falls straight down. The eaves will protect the plants much of the time and occasional rainfall blown into the bed won't hurt—even cacti need some moisture.

Certain fleshy and bulbous types of plants go dormant in the winter, and too much water then will kill them whether it gets cold or not. Small plastic panels or boards placed over them will keep their immediate environment dry, also planting them in pure sand will help keep water drained away from the bulb.

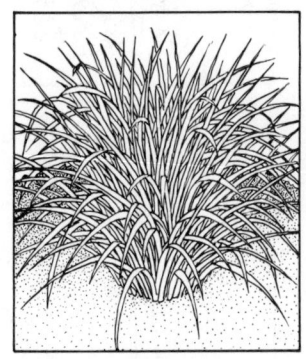

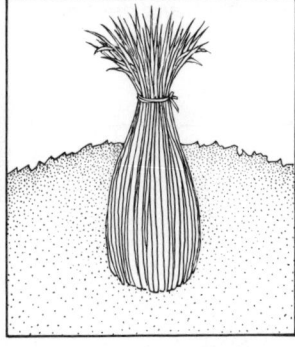

Many of the bulbous plants in the lily, amaryllis, and iris families get very clumpy and tend to rot in the winter. You can prevent this by simply tying the tops of the plant together.

Helping the Plants Survive 17

Quick Coverings for Winter

There are innumerable, imaginative schemes for protecting your plants against frost and heavy rain. Most plants need only a cover, but some will need heat also. Even in winter our days get quite warm, so be prepared to remove your covering or have a vent in it to let out the heat. Remember, too, that bare plastic touching foliage will cause the touching parts to freeze in cold weather. Structures can be as simple as a blanket thrown over a bush or as elaborate as a portable greenhouse.

If you've got your plants in rows, you can stake a cord above the plants and suspend newspapers over it. Newspapers are held to the ground by bricks.

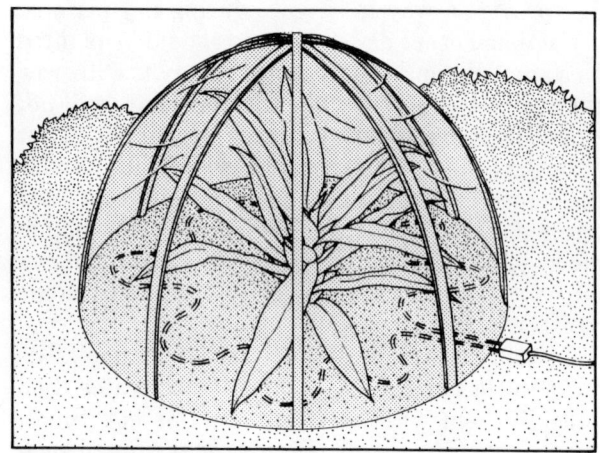

Quick protection for your favorites—a buried heating cable and a small wooden frame covered with plastic . . .

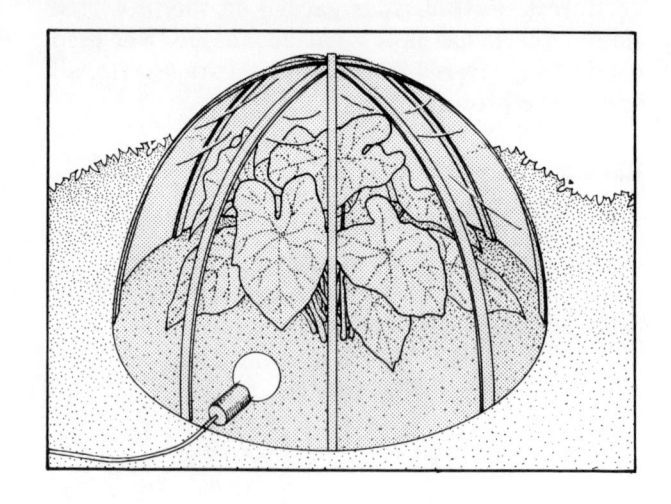

. . . you can also use a 60-watt light bulb, and the frame can be as simple as you like, just as long as it keeps the plastic off the plants.

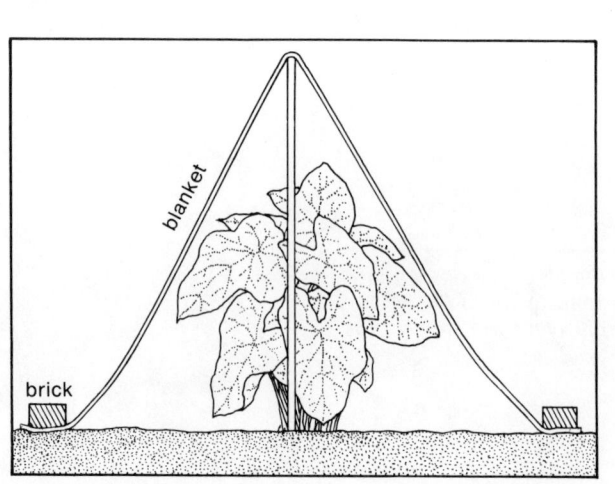

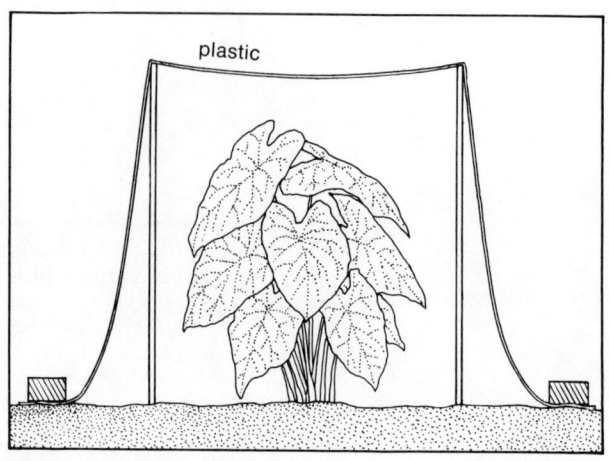

Simply supporting a blanket over your plants with a stake (left) is one of the best ways to protect your tropicals. You can use plastic (right), but this requires more support, since any part of the plant that touches the plastic will freeze.

18   Winter Coverings

(Above): An open-rafter patio can easily be converted to a temporary greenhouse by stapling polyethylene plastic to the frame. Reinforcement with meshed wire will make the patio look a bit neater and keep the cold plastic from touching the leaves of the plants. (Right): A quick greenhouse—2 x 4's nailed to the side and eave of the house. Tack on plastic, then staple on chicken wire. Sunshine outside and heat radiating from the house walls provide protective warmth.

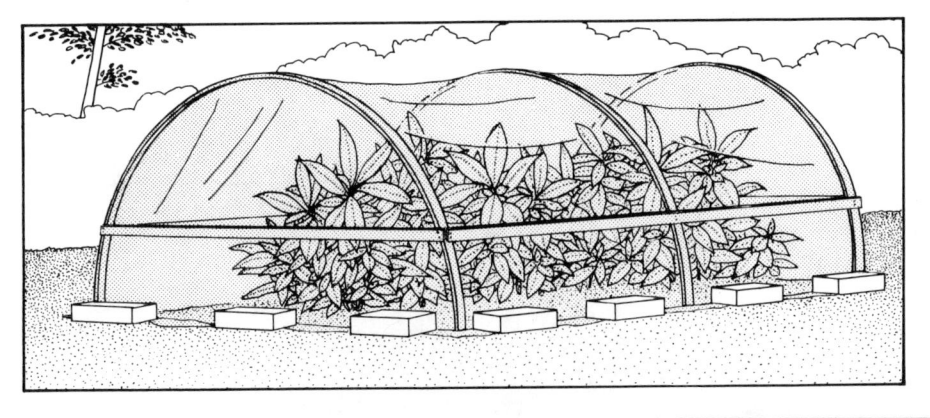

A quick and easy freestanding greenhouse. Simply bend 2'' x ¼'' x 12' strips of lattice over the plants and plunge them into the ground on either side. Then throw plastic over this instant frame and secure with bricks. A lateral piece nailed to each of these bent strips will provide extra support.

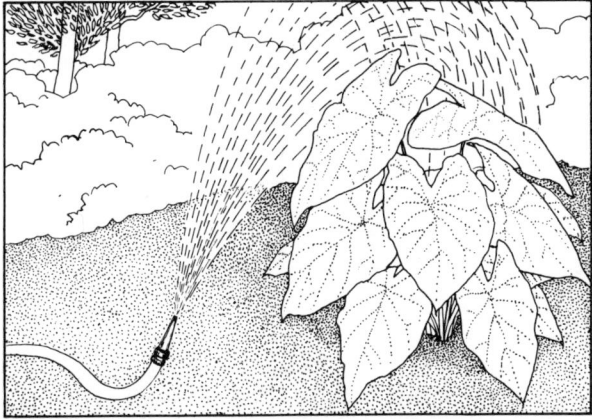

If it's only going to be a light freeze (to 30°) you can set a sprinkler on your plants to keep frost off; if it gets much colder than this, your garden will be covered with ice.

Winter Coverings

Heat

Heat is a problem only with a few tropicals. Occasionally we try to grow plants that come from the cool tropics, and for a period each summer these plants will suffer. Plants known to suffer from the summer heat should be placed on the east side of the house or on the north or east side of a larger shrub or tree. Planting in areas where there is air movement and readily available water also helps. A brief spray of water in the late afternoon will do much to lower the leaf temperatures.

Avoid planting heat-sensitive plants near sidewalks, along south walls, or in a full summer sun exposure. The morning sun is usually bright and cool; the afternoon sun is usually excessively hot. Place heat-sensitive specimens where they get overhead shade all summer and sunlight angled onto them in the winter. This is a good way to provide light and coolness too. Garden pools, especially those that are at least partially shaded, offer a cool respite for sensitive plants. Overhead lath structures that provide mid-day shade but do not obstruct air flow are also very useful.

Drought

Drought is one of our more perplexing problems. Droughts don't follow a predictable pattern in our area. After weeks of rain, a drought can occur for several weeks at *any* time of the year.

Elevated beds of humus-filled soil, surrounded by small irrigation ditches are a great value during droughts as well as deluges. It's simple to flood the ditch, and the humus helps to move the water through the bed, by capillary action.

Certain species require constant moisture. These should be planted near a pool, fountain, or other water source. Keeping excessive water users in check by pruning helps to keep the soil moisture up. And, for the zealous gardener, a sprinkler system is a great help.

For irrigating the garden, drip irrigation systems are becoming popular, especially in drier zones to the west of our area, but I feel that along the Gulf Coast they aren't worth the expense of installation and maintenance. We usually only have a drought for a few weeks once a year or so. It seems foolish to spend so much for a system that waters only the roots of your plants, when a spray head will be easier to use and provides important atmospheric moisture and cooling for your summertime tropical garden.

In some parts of the South the concentration of dissolved salts in the water supply is quite high. If the concentration is above 1,000 parts per million (check with your local Extension agent to find out), only water the roots, not the foliage: the salts can burn the leaves.

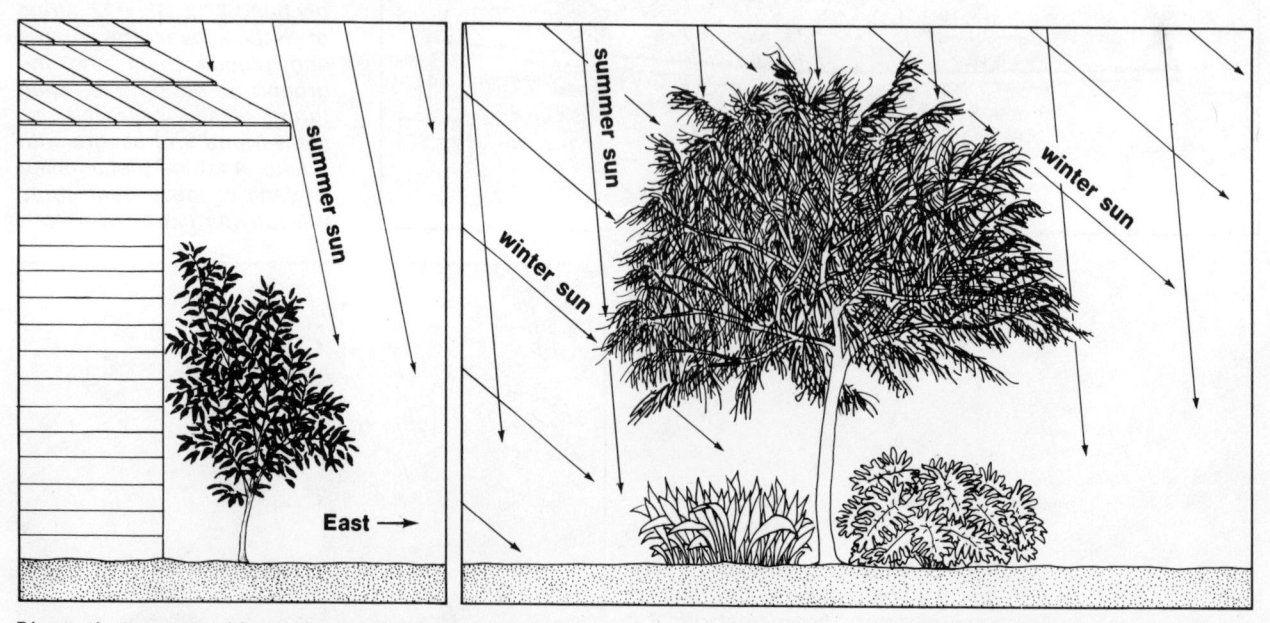

Plants that are sensitive to heat can be placed next to an east-facing wall of the home (left) to receive gentle morning sun and protection from the strong afternoon sun. You can also place these plants under a larger tree with a fairly deep root system (right). This will protect them from scorching summer sun yet allow them to receive the more angled, gentle fall and winter sun.

The Hardy, the Half-Hardy, and the Tender

For the southern regions covered by this book, I have devised a slightly different scheme of hardiness. All our discussions will be relative to zone 9 of the USDA hardiness map (see page iii). If you live north of this zone, you'll have to take steps to winter-protect *all* the plants listed. In this book the term *hardy* denotes tropical plants that are completely hardy in the Gulf Coast area. These plants do not freeze back or do so only slightly in very cold winters. Also included are hardy deciduous species that requre no special attention here in the way of winter protection.

The *half-hardy* plants are those tropicals that will survive here, but frost will damage or kill their above-ground portions. However, the plants will fully recover in the spring without any special help. If you choose to protect these plants, they will get through without any loss of leaves. In this way the plants will survive all but our most severe winters without any permanent damage.

The last group, *tender* plants, will be killed or nearly killed without some winter protection in northern parts of our zone. Because they are not hardy, only a few of these plants are included here. Several plants are included because they are either highly ornamental, easy to protect, or are common in our gardens in spite of it all.

Hardy

Acuba japonica
Agave sp.
Albizzia julibrissin
Amaryllis hallii
Aralia papyrifera
Araucaria bidwillii
Asparagus sprengeri
Aspidistra elatior
Bambusa sp.
Brunfeldia calycina
Butia
Callistemon sp.
Casurina equisetifolia
Catalpa speciosa
Chamaerops humilis
Cinnamonum camphora
Cortaderia selloana
Cycas revoluta
Cynara scolymus
Cyrtomium falcatum
Dicksonia antarctica
Dioon edule
Eriobotrya
Eucalyptus sp.
Fatsia japonica
Ficus carica
Ficus pumila
Firmiana simplex
Gardenia jasminioides
Graptopetalum paraguayense
Hedra sp.
Hymenocallis
Korkolwiczia sp.
Lagerstroemia indica
Lantana
Liriope
Livistonia chinensis
Marsilia sp.
Melia azedarach
Nephrolepis exaltata
Nerium oleander
Nymphaea
Onoclea sesibilis
Ophiopogon
Osmunda sp.
Parkinsonia aculeata
Phormium sp.
Plumbago
Punica granatum
Raphiolepis indica
Sabal sp.
Salix sp.
Trachelospermum jasminioides
Trachycarpus fortunei
Vitex
Washingtonia sp.
Yucca aloifolia

Half-Hardy

Adiantum cappillus veneris
Agapanthus sp.
Alocasia macrorrhiza
Aloe vera
Alpinia sp.
Araucaria araucana
Asparagus plumosus
Asparagus retrofractus
Bauhinia sp.
Beleperone guttata
Bougainvillea sp.
Callisia elegams
Canna indica
Carica papaya
Carissa grandiflora
Chlorophyllum comosum
Citrus sp.
Cocos plumosa
Colocasia esculenta
Cyperus alternifolius
Cyperus papyrus
Dioscorea sp.
Erythrina crista-galli
Euphorbia pulcherrima
Ficus decora
Gerbera jamesii
Hedychium coronarium
Hippestrum sp.
Jacobinia carnea
Musa sp.
Passiflora sp.
Persera americana
Philodendron sp.
Raphis excelsa
Strelizia sp.
Sultana impatians
Syngonium podophyllum
Tabernaemontana grandiflora
Tradiscantia sp.
Victoria regina
Xanthosoma sagittifolium
Zantedeschia sp.
Zebrina pendula

Tender

Acalypha wilkesiana
Allamanda
Alsophila australis
Araucaria excelsa
Bromeliaceae
Cacti
Caladium bicolor
Codiaeum variegatum
Coleus blumei
Heliconia sp.
Hibiscus rosa-sinensis
Monstera deliciosa
Orchidaceae
Plumeria sp.
Pothos scandens

Putting Your Tropical Garden Together

How to Begin

Careful planning and thoughtful design are what distinguish the appealing, interesting gardens from the ordinary, lackluster ones. All the plants in a tropical garden may be in the "pink" of condition, but if the esthetics are not there the real value of the garden is lost. There are many fine books covering all aspects of landscaping. My intention here is not to compete with them but to point out a few things that you might overlook and to offer some suggestions as you plan your tropical garden.

Location

Before you begin to plant your tropical garden, decide where you will place it. This decision, more than any other, will govern your choice of plants.

In the more northerly parts of zone 9 it is extremely important to place your garden in a protected area. As mentioned earlier, south- and east-facing walls are more protected than north- or west-facing walls. The eastern exposure is the most protected from hot afternoon sun, drying west winds, and "blue northers"; the western exposure is the least protected from these.

In order of desirability then, the eastern exposure is best followed by the hotter, dryer southern exposure. The full northern exposure is less desirable than the southern, but it doesn't get the hot west sun, so it too has an advantage over the western exposure.

A protected entryway is better than one straight wall, and the relative advantages of each entryway exposure are the same: east is best, west is worst. The same is true for walls, fences, garages, etc. The east side is best even if the garden is planted away from the wall a few feet.

In the more southerly parts of our area, of course, the climate is more moderate and the importance of exposure is less, but it's still significant. Gardens should get 4 to 6 hours of sun. Therefore, dense overhead trees can cause a shading problem. But if you grow shade-loving plants, the overhead trees are no imposition (see page 77). Throughout our area the sun arcs far enough to the north and high enough in the sky that almost every surface that isn't directly under a tree will get some sun for part of the year.

The location of soil types may be another constraint. If you have a band of loam soil in a yard otherwise filled with clay, of course that spot is the better location for your garden. Terrain is another

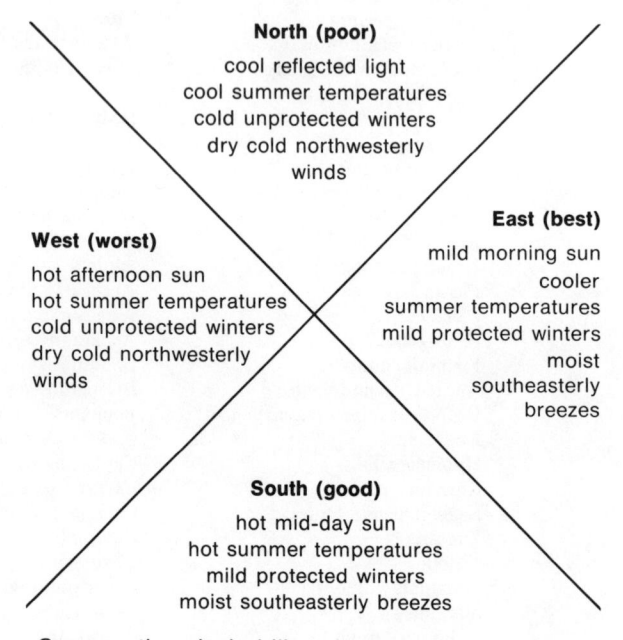

North (poor)
cool reflected light
cool summer temperatures
cold unprotected winters
dry cold northwesterly winds

West (worst)
hot afternoon sun
hot summer temperatures
cold unprotected winters
dry cold northwesterly winds

East (best)
mild morning sun
cooler summer temperatures
mild protected winters
moist southeasterly breezes

South (good)
hot mid-day sun
hot summer temperatures
mild protected winters
moist southeasterly breezes

Comparative desirability of exposures for tropical plants: east is best, west is worst.

consideration: it's easy to water dry plants, but it is very difficult to drain excessive soil water off a low spot when it rains.

Plans

Plan your garden before you plant it. Set it up on grid paper and plot out the mature sizes of all plants so you'll know just where everything goes. Place all access ways, work areas, walls, buried electrical lines, water lines, etc. on the drawing. Make all your drawings the same scale, i.e., ¼ inch equals 1 foot.

Be honest about the *mature* sizes of all your plants. Now is the time to overcome potential problems of crowded or underplanted spots. Put the approximate bloom dates on each plant depicted to determine if your garden will have overall color throughout the year. Think about the dormancy of certain plants. Some species die down in the summer, others die down in the winter. It is very embarrassing to hide a garden work center behind a clump of bananas and discover that next fall all is in full view because the bananas froze to the ground. And take your time! Your garden will only be as good as your plan.

Landscaping with Tropical Plants

The kinds of garden areas you may consider fall into a variety of categories, each of which has its own peculiarities. These categories include garden-type plantings, protected entryways, atriums, patios, and pool sides. Let's look briefly at each.

Gardens

A lush tropical garden with pathways and secluded garden seats is a common vision to many gardeners. The area encompassed by such a garden need not even be very extensive, but it takes planning and forethought to attain the proper effect.

Avoid heavily shaded areas. Try to structure your garden to avoid straight-sided beds; free-form curves have tremendous eye appeal. Giving the garden a layered effect will provide a feeling of depth, even in a small yard. Normally, gardens are tapered so the tallest plants are to the rear and shorter plants to the fore. Tropical gardens are fre-

A curving, free-form planting. By placing taller plants to the back, shorter ones to the front, you can provide a feeling of depth, even in a small yard. Represented here (clockwise from left back row) are: hibiscus, rice paper plant, manihot, bamboo, banana, New Zealand flax, umbrella plant (with heliconia behind), liriope (with tree fern and spider plant behind), philodendron, and bird of paradise. Water lilies float in foreground garden pool.

A corner of the house is a good spot for a tropical garden, especially if one side faces east. The border of this garden is asparagus fern, backed up (from left to right) by aucubas, caladiums, philodendron, fatsia, and blood banana.

quently established in the same way, but to achieve a real tropical effect, place a couple of tall accent plants well forward so the viewer is required to walk beneath the foliage as in a jungle.

I always try to place a strong-growing, tallish plant with upright lines at the corners of my beds. In so doing, I can visually extend my garden well beyond the limits of each path. It also removes the temptation to cut the corners off your garden and make short-cuts through it. Lastly, sooner or later the garden will need water, and hoses tend to wreck short plants.

For esthetic as well as practical reasons, raised beds are a real advantage: in addition to providing good drainage and allowing you a chance to fill the beds with a proper soil mix, raised beds make the plants more visible, giving easily overlooked small plants a chance to be seen.

An open, grassy area next to the garden will lend the feeling of depth and add considerably to the garden's natural demeanor. Every garden should have a pool of some sort. If possible, situate it in an area where half the pool can get full sun and half partial shade. This way you'll be able to grow any of your favorite water plants.

Those of you with pet dogs may consider leaving a 2- or 3-foot wide pathway along your fence. This pathway serves the dual purpose of access to the

A long and narrow tropical garden along one side of the home. Illustrated here are (from front): variegated liriope, cast iron plant, and umbrella plant.

24 Landscaping with Tropical Plants

back of the garden and allowing your curious pet an opportunity to check out the fence without tramping down the flowers. And children can chase down stray balls etc. without tearing up the garden. Lastly, nearly all gardeners plant large plants too close to the fence, only to regret it later. Big plants break down fences, but with your path suitably placed, this problem doesn't arise. Don't forget garden lights. They will bring out highlights and let you enjoy many more hours in the garden on cool evenings.

Protected Entryways

Entryways, especially those that are fully enclosed, have the protection, size and setting that are ideal for a stunning tropical garden, and their small size offers a compact area in which to concentrate your effort. The back walls and walkways limit your view angles, making it much easier to landscape than an atrium, while the protection allows you more versatility in your choice of tropicals.

The drawbacks to protected entryways are the frequently poor light availability of north-facing entryways and the size problems you may encounter with certain of the larger-growing bananas, philodendrons, and bamboos. Many of the tropicals discussed in this book have dwarf or small-growing counterparts which are eminently suitable. Such plants as dwarf Indian hawthorne, the blood banana, windmill palm, caladiums, impatiens, dwarf New Zealand flax, the Tasmanian tree fern, and others will be ideal for the protected entryway.

Atriums

Many newer homes have atriums designed right in. Ideally, the atrium will be big enough and the surrounding wall short enough to allow direct sunlight to reach the ground all year. But not all designs are this favorable. Atriums are often glass-walled on all sides, which means that every side is a viewing side. There is no front side or back side to these types, so they are a real challenge.

Most atriums tend to be rather small and dark. In these cases the conservation of overhead light becomes essential. There must be a water source in the atrium; you don't want to drag a muddy hose

A protected entrance to the home is an ideal spot. Left side, back row (from front): New Zealand flax, Norfolk Island pine, philodendron; middle row: impatiens alternated with bird of paradise. Right side, back row (from front): heliconia, tree fern, bird of paradise; center row: jacobinia. Caladiums border both sides of the walkway.

Entryways and Atriums

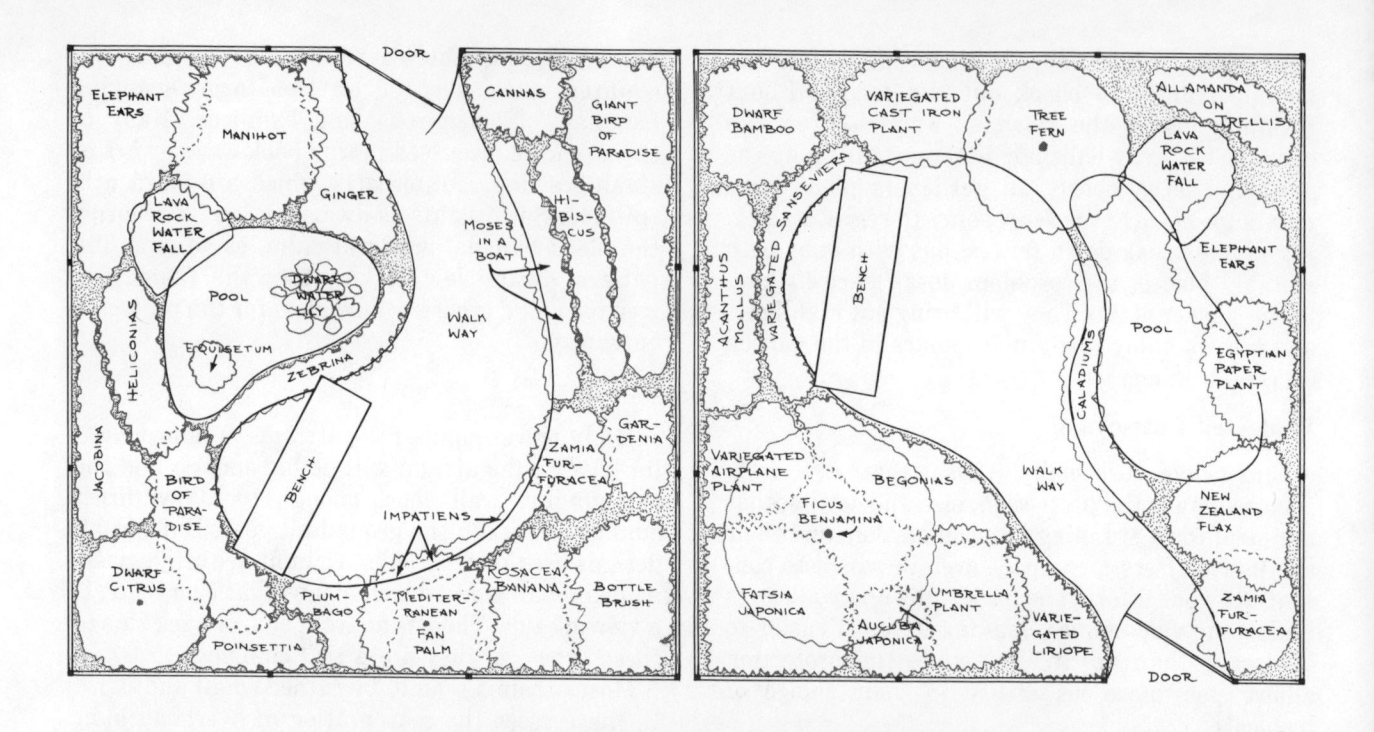

Possibilities for a sunny atrium (top left) and a shady atrium (top right). Immediately above is a design for an atrium surrounded by windows, with doorways on three sides. The plants represented here are all hardy and will be attractive for eight to nine months out of the year. Left foreground: manihot, variegated spider plant, spider lily, rice paper plant. Right foreground: umbrella plant, variegated liriope, fatsia, blood banana, crapemyrtle, and holly fern. Background: sago palm, rosacea banana, acanthus, wind mill palm, and impatiens.

Atrium Gardens

through the house. You'll also have to provide some drainage. Soil levels should be kept well below the entryway levels. The soil should be porous, so add sand and gravel. French drains may also be necessary if water frequently collects and the soil is a very non-porous clay.

Walkways should be of a very coarse gravel that won't be tracked into the house; even better would be a slightly elevated board walk or central pathway with a pebbled or rough-textured surface to prevent slipping. Stepping stones work well, but they too should have a textured surface.

If your atrium has limited light, avoid planting too many tall tree-like specimens, since they will cut out what light there is. Concentrate on shorter foliage types with good leaf design and color variation. For the excessively sunny atrium, tall specimens are a real asset since they serve to filter the light.

Most atriums are open to the sky but are otherwise well protected from wind and frost. The immediate proximity of the house provides winter heat, so many half-hardy and tender plants can be attempted that might otherwise fail in your section of the South.

Occasionally, people make permanent (but vented) plexiglass covers for their atriums. These, of course, allow you to plant any tropical you like. But remember, some of the warm temperate plants we treat as tropicals may not appreciate the total protection afforded by a year-round enclosed atrium. Some of these plants may do poorly.

Other people make temporary covers for winter. These, too, need to be vented on warm damp days. Beyond the fact that they are removed in the summer, there are no practical differences between these and the permanent covers with regard to cultivation except that the temporary ones get summer showers, the permanently enclosed structures don't.

Patios and Planters

Landscaped patios are extremely popular these days, and if you stick some free-standing or elevated planters and a lath cover out there, you can really go to town creating a tropical patio. The planters may be of redwood, cedar, cement or terra cotta. They may be large or small.

Since so much attention will be focused on the planters, it's important to choose your specimens very carefully. If you have a tendency to forget to water them, you must use agaves or other dry-growing plants that will forgive occasional dry spells. On the other hand, the armament of an agave can be intimidating. Likewise, patio shading can be harmful to sun-loving plants, while shade-loving philodendrons may burn with too much light. So, pick your plants carefully. You want plants that can withstand your patio's light, water, and exposure. Further, the plant must be distinctive. It would be a pity to have some nondescript plant in such a focal point. Ideal choices are plumeria, split-leaf philodendron, jathropa, hibiscus, bamboo, and pony tail palm.

You can put your tropicals in planters and make a jungle out of the patio. A lath cover is just perfect for hanging baskets and vines.

A built-in planter along one side or at the back of the patio is always attractive. If your patio is an open-rafter type, a built-in planter at the rear, near the house, is ideal. But if your patio is a solid-roof type, it will probably cut out too much light for healthy plant growth, so use planters on rollers. This way the plants can be rolled into the sunshine.

Your planters must drain at the base. Fill them with rich, loamy soil and choose your plants carefully. Pay particular attention to the mature sizes of each plant you use; don't crowd them. I suggest avoiding woody shrubs and vines. Neither group seems to work in patio planters, with the exception of hibiscus, certain ficus, alamanda, and

grow. Tender plants also can be put into the garden for the summer and placed in protected areas all winter. Planters and individual decorative pots are useful for poolsides and patios where you have no ground beds.

Certain plants especially useful or spectacular as potted specimens are plumeria, elk horn euphorbia, pony tail palms.

Swimming Pools

Swimming pools and tropical plants are a very natural combination. With a little care in planting and positioning of garden lights, a landscaped swimming pool area can be the high spot of any home.

Be creative with your planters—the growth habits and characteristics of your tropical plants are diverse, and your containers should be, too.

bougainvillea. Keep all trimmed and in bounds and they'll do well in outdoor planters. Other candidates not already mentioned are bamboo, selloum philodendron, and wandering jew.

Potted Plants. Potted plants are always useful for mobile color. They are ideal to brighten dark corners because they can be moved to the sun to

Most pools are surrounded by a wide deck of concrete that is singularly unappealing. To offset the stark quality of this concrete, large planters with tropical plants can be placed to advantage at strategic points around the pool. You can also use a variety of plants that will hang out over the decking, providing a soothing contrast to the concrete.

Bamboos and ferns lend an authentic, overgrown tropical look to the courtyard or patio.

A narrow or curving decking will allow more appealing, fulsome "islands" of green surrounding the pool. By planting tiers of tropicals in each island, you can create a flow of vegetation that surrounds the pool with delightful greenery.

All these planting spots should be treated as small gardens. Each should include proper soil drainage, etc., with all normal horticultural practices taken into account. One delightful aspect of tropicals is their tendency *not* to drop leaves in the water. Most tropicals have large leaves that remain connected or at least don't blow around. (Bamboo and hibiscus are two exceptions.)

Don't plant bamboo or bananas too close to the cement; both will buckle the concrete if they are cramped by it.

Many gardeners worry that the swimming pool chlorine will hurt the plants. While strong doses of chlorine aren't healthy for tropicals, this infrequent problem is minor compared to normal problems of a lack of water, food, and light. In short, if your plants are kept healthy and are treated normally, chlorine will do no appreciable harm.

Garden Pools

An authentic tropical garden really should have some kind of standing or running water. Your garden pool may be as small as a split barrel with water in it, a small plastic garden pool, or a larger goldfish pond. The choice is endless, and whole books have been written on the subject.

You can grow water lilies in a small pool in partial shade. The light is bright yet subdued enough to support the lily and discourage algae.

Lilies like at least 8 inches of water over their crowns, so your pool should be at least 1 foot deep. A variety of interesting water plants can be grown: dwarf water lilies, Egyptian paper plants, water hyacinths, water shields, and horse tails, among others.

How about water fountains and waterfalls? Small pumping units are readily available locally and by mail-order. I am very partial to waterfalls with water trickling down a log or lava rock. Both fountains and falls contribute a great deal to cooling the garden and keeping it humid. They are always a superb addition.

Fish and turtles are also lots of fun, especially for kids. Don't catch your own, though. Wild fish carry diseases and frequently will eat all the other fish in the pool if given the chance. Goldfish, koi, and other pool fish are always available and are usually inexpensive.

Pathways

For larger gardens, pathways are a necessity. They may be constructed of wood blocks, gravel, bark chips, bricks, or left alone as grass.

Any pathway should be wide enough to accommodate its designated use. If your path goes to and from work areas, give it room. Four to six feet wide is best. Of course, if all you need is a path to the rear of the garden, two to three feet wide is suitable. But remember, plants will always be overhanging the path, so make it too wide rather than too narrow. The plants will happily overgrow it.

Try not to make straight pathways—they're very dull. If your garden has soft lines, give your path curves; if your garden has strict lines, then give your path angular bends. But don't let it be

Curved plantings around the swimming pool create a flowing, soothing contrast to the concrete decking, enhance privacy, and embellish the pool area with greenery.

Garden pools and tropical plants complement each other perfectly.

30 **Swimming Pools, Garden Pools**

Tips on Garden Pools

Before you install or construct a pool for the garden, think twice about where to put it. The pool should get partial to full sun if you are going to grow water lilies or other flowering water plants. The pool's water depth should vary from 6 inches to 2 feet. This way, shallow emergent plants can be grown along with the water lilies, which need deeper water to develop properly.

Nothing is more aggravating than a pool without a drain or a way to remove the water easily. Water may be removed by a siphon if a down slope is nearby. Otherwise, a drain hooked into the sewer or to a surface outlet will work well. Make reasonable provisions from the start—bailing out a pool is hard work.

Plumbing and electrical connections for fountains, etc., should be installed first and in such a way that they are readily accessible. Digging up a pool to fix a broken line is just no fun at all.

Water weighs a great deal and puts stress on your pool, so build it strong, preferably from reinforced concrete at least 3 inches thick. Small pools of prefabricated plastic are o.k., but don't make them out of polyethylene film. It will leak, the plastic will break down, and a great deal of time and effort will be wasted.

Keep the pool filled all year. In our area ground water will fill in under an empty pool and pop it out of the ground. It is quite distressing to see your empty garden pool floating about in your backyard!

Fish are an inexpensive way to keep mosquitoes from breeding in your pool. Most pools are sufficiently large to provide enough insects for a few fish, so you won't have to feed them. In our area most fish are completely hardy since the water never freezes solid.

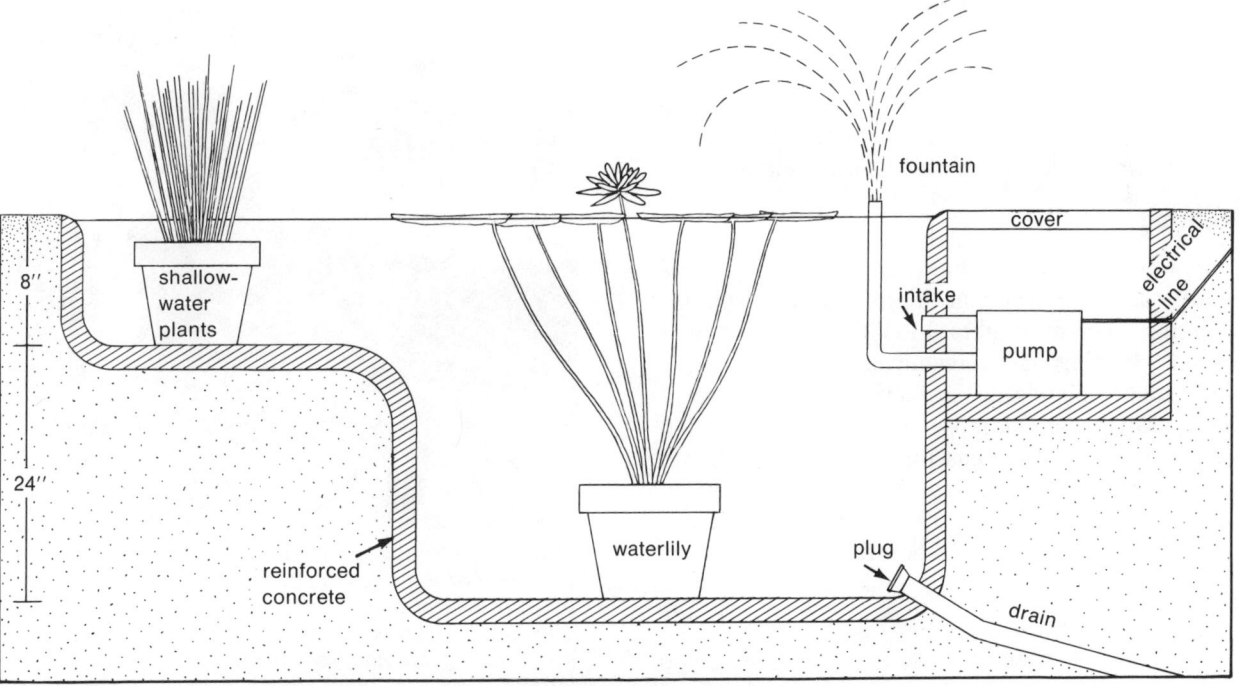

A typical design for a garden pool. By varying the depth of the pool, you can grow shallow emergent plants, such as water hyacinths and waterpoppies, as well as water lilies, which require 2 feet of water.

straight. Try to slope them slightly so water drains off the path, not to it. It is also useful to have the surface of your path raised an inch or so above the surrounding ground so it will drain well during wet weather.

Wall, Screens and Fences

In a region as uniformly flat as ours, walls, screens, and fences provide the only relief we have from a monotonous landscape. Each can be used to advantage in the garden. Work areas must be hidden, privacy must be preserved. Judicious use of these partitions can give the illusion of space in a small area. They can add interest and character to the garden. Trailing plants can be planted atop them, and baskets can be hung from them.

Bridges

Bridges can be used only in larger gardens. They may be used to cross a small pond or landscaped over a dry rock stream bed. Some of my more fortunate readers will need them to cross a ravine on their property. Bridges can liven a dull pathway.

Furniture

The right furniture lends utility and beauty to the garden. Furniture, more than any other garden addition, allows you to relax and enjoy the plants—and that's the point of it all: enjoyment. No garden should be all toil and no fun.

Benches, chaises, tables, and chairs are a must if the garden is to be the restful, relaxing creation you intended. These furnishings make the garden inviting, hospitable. Without them, the garden just sits out there like an exhibit in a museum.

Lighting

By supplying electric lighting, you can enjoy the beauty of the garden at night and play up interesting color highlights. Floodlights played on a cluster planting of philodendron or swiss cheese plant make a striking attraction in the dark of night. "Mushroom" lamps softly lighting a garden pathway are another possibility. Lighting should be used to accent pools, spots of color, pathways, and the like. The fixtures themselves should be unobtrusive and concealed if possible.

Focal Points

Since your garden is predominantly green, you should consider the development of colorful focal points. A bed of cannas, impatiens or hibiscus can contribute intense color to the overwhelming greenness of the garden. Foliage plants, too, can add color in the form of variegated hibiscus, caladium or a cluster of blood bananas. Textured foliage, as that of selloum philodendron or the various elephant ears, deserves consideration.

Keep your focal plantings simple. A clustered planting destroys the entire idea.

Ornamental lamps help make the garden more than just a daytime enjoyment. Soft lighting and shadows play up the engaging color highlights and shapes of the plants.

Most of the tropical plants are all-green, but you can give the garden a feeling of fullness and diversity by playing off the plants' varying leaf textures against one another. Look at the contrasts in this garden: erect young banana foliage in center, with gently curving cast iron plant leaves nestled to the right. At left in background, a fan palm relieves all the softness with its spiny leaves. In the center foreground, shade-loving impatiens grows beneath all this; air potato vine climbs above.

Tropical Plants for the Gulf Coast

In this section over 150 species of plants are alphabetically presented for possible inclusion in your tropical garden. I've included representatives of all plant types, from trees and shrubs to vines and herbaceous plants. With each plant listed is a description, a discussion of its desirable aspects, cultivation requirements, uses in the garden, interesting cultivars, and possible problems.

One of my major problems was deciding what to include. The list here is culled from an initial list of over 300 species. Obviously, many favorite plants have been left out. This book is not intended as an encyclopedia; rather, I want to show the possibilities for the tropical gardener in the South. For this reason some very common plants as well as some very obscure ones are included.

You'll find "tropical-looking" as well as genuinely tropical plants in this section. And you'll be able to think of dozens of other prospects for your tropical garden. From the facts about the plants included here, you can project the requirements and success of other plants you may wish to try.

Many plants have several common names and often several botanical names. I have tried to use well-known common names for each species. Wherever possible and reasonable, I have tried to be botanically correct, but on occasion it was necessary to use a traditional name since the real botanical name is so obscure no one would recognize it.

This listing is arranged alphabetically by botanical names, which are in boldface type. Common names are in italics, and the botanical names of plants sub-listed under a family are in regular Roman type.

Most plants continue to get larger throughout their lives. The "mature" sizes are often hard to determine. Therefore, I have quoted sizes that I have actually seen the plants get in normal gardens. I realize that individuals may be larger or smaller at times; I have tried to present the most typical size a plant obtains.

Acalypha wilkesiana
Copper Plant

The copper plant is one of those plants that is ideally suited to southern gardens. It is fast-growing, extremely colorful, and loves the heat, sun, and long summers of our region. Several forms of the plant are cultivated. Cuttings are planted in mid-spring in rich, well drained soil with full sun. By fall, bushes up to 4 feet tall will develop that are clothed in large 6-inch copper-colored leaves which last until frost.

The plant is easy to grow if it gets enough sun and warmth. It is particularly useful because of the striking color of the foliage, but its demand for sun to help it color up is a problem for those with shady yards. The copper plant is quite tender, freezing with the first frost, and does not like the cool early days of spring or late fall. If you have a greenhouse, cuttings are over-wintered easily; otherwise it's probably better to purchase small plants each spring, treating the copper plant as our northern friends treat their garden geraniums.

Adiantum capillus-veneris
Maidenhair Fern

The maidenhair fern is many gardeners' first love. It is also one of the most perplexing plants to grow. Gardeners everywhere love its soft green fronds borne on viney, black stems, yet every time they try to grow it, it dies. The problem is easily solved: It seems that maidenhair ferns are adapted to wet alkaline places, *not* wet acid places. In nature, maidenhairs grow on dripping limestone cliffs! To grow it one needs to add limestone to the soil, keep it damp to wet, and all will be well. The maidenhair is completely hardy everywhere in our area, and once you know about the water and limestone requirement, it's easy to grow.

Agapanthus sp.
Lily of the Nile

Agapanthus provides us with lovely small blue or white lily-like flowers in early summer. These develop out of a typical lily-like plant composed of clusters of many narrow, green, curved leaves. The plant gets about 15 inches tall, with flowers above that.

Cultivation is the same as for other lilies: a sandy, well-drained soil, lots of 6-10-4 fertilizer to encourage flowers, and sun. It is quite hardy, dying to the ground each fall and returning each spring. However, it is sensitive to sogging conditions. Give it lots of sand so excess water will drain away and not rot the bulbs.

Agapanthus albidus
White Lily of the Nile

Similar to blue lily of the Nile, A. albidus bears lovely white flowers. It is not seen as frequently, but it offers a lovely contrast to the blue form and the two work well planted together in a large mixed flower bed.

Agapanthus orientalis
Blue Lily of the Nile

This is the common blue form. It also comes in a dwarf version. It establishes well but needs good drainage to avoid rot.

Agave sp.

The agaves all hail from portions of the New World, but their striking form, size, and "survivability" have endeared them to gardeners the world over. While they are desert plants, agaves will succeed wherever it is sunny and warm and the soil is well drained.

Along the Gulf Coast they do just fine. They are tolerant of salty sea spray, wind, hot exposures, and even the clay gumbo soils and occasional severe frosts we get. Always plant them in sunny sites, however. Agaves grown in the shade develop poorly and look horrible. Try to provide a sandy soil for them, or at least put a bucket or two of sand at the base of each plant to help drain the rain and soil moisture away from the crown. Also, it helps if you plant them on a slight mound to improve drainage. The plants are ideal for west walls, dry corners near entryways, and around light posts. For those who have a Spanish-style home agaves are almost a necessity to set it off.

Remember one thing: agaves, especially A. americana, will get huge, so give them room. Plant them at least 8 feet from walkways and traffic areas. Each leaf is armed with many curved spines on the margins and a substantial terminal thorn on the end. As for pests, well, almost no insect will bother them and I assure you that no people will either; they are tough and beautiful.

There are a vast array of interesting agaves; I will mention the two most popular here.

Agave americana
Century Plant

A. americana, its varieties, and a few other species that masquerade as this plant, are all large, tolerant plants that require little care or attention. The silvery leaves of A. americana regularly get 5 feet long at maturity, so give them a lot of room or be prepared to move them (a difficult job) in a few years. Many forms of A. americana have been cultivated; I will discuss three.

The typical americana has wide silver leaves, black thorns, and flowers every 10-20 years (not once a century). The flowering stalk gets 20-30 feet tall and resembles a green telephone pole. After flowering, the plant dies, but many suckers

Agave americana.

develop and soon as one plant dies away a large new clump develops after a few years.

Two other forms are grown, depending upon where you are. The first is characterized by gray leaves that do not bend outward toward the tip of the leaf, giving the plant a very strict, straight appearance. The other form has leaves reflexed toward the tip, causing the plant to develop a much more stylized shape. This form and the typical americana are quite hardy throughout our area.

There also are variegated forms with green and yellow or green and white leaves that are much narrower than the typical A. americana. The variegated forms are prettiest when kept smaller, and they are less frost-tolerant than the typical. In especially bad winters they will freeze back, but they'll recover in the spring.

Agave attenuata

A. attenuata has soft yellow-green leaves without thorns. It is very ornamental, gets about 3 feet high, and sometimes develops a stem. It needs soil with good drainage, good sun, and some protection in winter. Otherwise, the leaves may spot badly or the plant may freeze. This highly ornamental agave is worth the effort to grow.

Albizzia julibrissin
Mimosa

The mimosa must be the most commonly planted small tree in the South. It quickly forms a flat-topped 20-foot tree covered with fine foliage and clusters of powderpuff pink flowers in early summer. The tree's very quick growth (branches sometimes grow 8 feet a year) and lovely flowers are reason enough for its popularity.

Mimosa prefers full sun and lots of fertilizer and water to do well. It is hardy throughout our area. One problem is that the plant likes to branch very low. To prevent this, frequent pruning to remove all lower branches is necessary (otherwise it will be impossible to mow the lawn beneath the tree).

The mimosa is an ideal specimen tree whose foliage provides light shade which allows the lawn to continue to grow.

Allamanda cathartica
Allamanda

The allamanda looks like a cartoon flower. Each flower is bright yellow with five big round petals fused together around a large yellow tube. Flowers are 3 inches or more across, last several days, and are produced all summer. The plant itself is really a slow-growing vine that produces whorls of glossy, lanceolate, evergreen leaves. Like so many other plants, the allamanda has only become popular recently, but it has been around for years.

Supposedly, allamanda is hardy here, but I prefer to treat it as a pot or tub plant and set it out in the garden in summer and keep it in a cool room of the touse all winter. Another undemanding plant, allamanda likes sun, normal potting soil, even moisture, and fertilizer once in a while.

It is a vine and can get large, but it is easily kept in bouds by trimming the occasional viney branches back to about 18 inches long. The flowers will develop out of the whorls of leaves, so trimming won't destroy future flowers.

Some people have succeeded in trellising allamandas on a south or east building wall, which can get the plants through most winters unharmed. Whether you keep it potted or plant it out, allamanda is certainly one of the really fine additions to the tropical garden.

A flower of the allamanda, a flowering vine for the trellis.

Aloe vera
Medicinal Aloe

With the current "health" and "back to nature" rage, Aloe vera has come into vogue as mother nature's answer to mosquito bites, bee stings, sunburn, scorched hands, etc. In addition, Aloe vera is a delightful if somewhat sensitive addition to the tropical garden. The plant comes from South Africa, as do most aloes, but is now found the world over on window shelves in temperate regions and in the garden in tropical areas.

A healthy Aloe vera will develop a fleshy-leaved rosette of light green leaves to about 2 feet tall and surrounded by smaller plants. Each summer a lovely spire of yellow tubular flowers is produced.

Cultivation is easy. Aloe vera requires sandy, well drained soil, not too much water, partial shade to full sun, and protection from severe frost in the winter. The plant is classed as half-hardy here since a hard freeze will kill the leaves. The aloe recovers from such freezes, but it takes 2-3 years to regain flowering size, so protect it or plant it near the house.

Aloe vera, a cactus that produces a natural ointment for skin irritations.

Alpina speciosa
Shell Ginger

The shell ginger is more interesting than pretty, producing tubular white flowers out of cone-like bracts. The plant itself gets up to 12 feet tall and has two ranks of long narrow leaves. It is less commonly seen than the butterfly ginger, but it should be treated in a similar way.

Shell ginger needs lots of water, light, food, and warmth to do well. It will stand some frost but normally freezes down in all but the most southern parts of zone 9.

The plant lacks great appeal and should be kept to the back of the tropical garden where the showy flowers can be seen but the plant is less obvious.

Flowering shell ginger.

Alsophila australis
Australian Tree Fern

The most popular of cultivated tree ferns is the Australian tree fern. It is a large plant, regularly getting 10 or more feet tall and spreading 8 or more feet wide. This tree fern is stunning in size and elegance and never fails to elicit comments from visitors.

In our area the plant is rather tender. It does not like freezes below 30°F, which severely limits its potential in unprotected areas. In entryways, atriums, and protected places, however, the plant has great utility. Like other ferns, it requires a humus soil, constant moisture, and shade. It should also be protected from the wind since its leaves are so large. For some, the size may be unwieldy, but if you have the room, it is a great plant.

Aralia papyrifera
Rice Paper Plant

If ever there was a tropical-looking temperate plant, the rice paper plant is it. The plant produces many gray-green, saucer-shaped leaves on a thick stem each year. It is slow-growing, but with a series of good years the plant will get up to 15 feet tall. Mature plants produce a huge, branched flower cluster each fall that is more unusual than beautiful.

The Chinese really do make rice paper from this plant. They beat the stem pith together into sheets to make the paper, a process which requires many plants.

Like so many other plants in this book, the rice paper plant will grow in sun or shade. I feel they develop better in the shade, protected from the hot sun and strong winds.

The plant is hardy here and usually begins the next year's growth on top of the previous year's to develop a tall but unbranched plant. Occasionally they will freeze to the ground, but small ones will develop quickly from the roots. The rice paper plant should be in every tropical garden.

Rice paper plant. Paper is made from the stems, not the leaves.

Araucaria sp.

Araucarias are tropical trees related to pine and spruce trees. Nearly all come from South America and the South Pacific, where there are entire forests of these enormous trees. In our area they do not get quite as big as they do in their native lands. Araucarias are not widely seen here, but they make fine specimen plants in a large yard. They also create a fine tall background planting in front of which shorter exotics can be placed. Araucarias add some unique textures to the tropical garden; they should be planted more often.

All araucarias prefer a sandy, acid soil and reasonable moisture. They are rather slow-growing compared to other tropicals but will still add 2 to 3 feet of height each year. Because of their slower growth, fertilizer should be applied in smaller amounts than with other tropicals.

Only three araucaria species are seen in our area with any frequency, two of these are reasonably hardy while the third is tender.

Araucaria araucana
Monkey Puzzle Tree

This very distinctive tree produces long branches that rebranch in a very geometric way, resembling a candelabra, and are clothed all the way around with many 1-inch long dark green narrow pointed leaves. The story is that the monkey puzzle tree gets its name from its spiney leaves which prevent monkeys from wrapping their tails around the branches when they climb, much to their puzzlement.

In mild winters the monkey puzzle tree is completely hardy, but during cold winters they may sustain some damage. Try to plant them near a wall or house where the tree can get at least house-high before it faces a hard winter. Monkey puzzle trees are hard to find in some sections of the Gulf Coast, but they are definitely worth searching for.

Araucaria bidwillii
Bunya Bunya

This is far more common and far more hardy than the monkey puzzle. From a distance the two look similar, except that the bunya bunya produces its pointed leaves in two ranks rather than all around the branch like the monkey puzzle. The bunya bunya is hardy throughout our area. I've seen large ones sustain freezes of 15° without damage. In protected locales the tree will easily get 30 or more feet tall and 20 feet wide with a wide dome-shaped crown.

Araucaria excelsa
Norfolk Island Pine

This tree grows in the South Pacific in the Norfolk Islands. It forms a large tree, 80 feet, and looks for all the world like a huge green candle. In our area the plant is severely retarded by frost and is usually treated as a houseplant. In coastal areas where frosts are rare and not too harsh the Norfolk Island pine will get 15 feet tall, and occasionally more, before it is too exposed to the elements to continue to survive the winters. It is probably best to plant these in protected entryways or atriums where their very handsome growth is shown to advantage and protection is available. Also, you can expect to replace your outdoor plants every few years. That's no problem since Norfolk Island pines are easily available and fairly inexpensive throughout the Gulf Coast area.

Arecastrum Romanzoffianum
Cocos Plumosa

Cocos plumosa is another very large palm. It can easily reach 30 or more feet in height, crowned by a plume of fluffy fronds. These distinctive fronds are composed of leaflets that radiate out of each side of the central leaf rib, causing the leaf to appear fluffy rather than fan or paddle-shaped. Cocos

Norfolk Island pine. In the South Pacific, this tree gets 80 feet tall; along the Gulf Coast, it will only grow to 15 feet.

plumosa is a very erect grower that holds its large leaves up rather than out, and this contributes to its overall tall appearance. The plant also is a quick-growing one, adding a couple of feet of stem height per year.

In the northern portions of zone 9 cocos plumosa is not dependably hardy. Severe winters will kill out most of those that are not well protected by a house or those that have outgrown their protection. In these areas it is necessary to replant cocos plumosa every few years if you want to maintain one. Further south in zone 9 cocos plumosas are quite hardy and are an important landscaping item. In the southerly areas they are planted in groups of three to five, which helps to offset the rather startling character of the plant.

Asparagus sp.

The asparagus ferns are not ferns at all but are members of the lily family and are closely related to the edible asparagus. All members of the genus have very fern-like foliage; hence the descriptive name. Unlike true ferns, however, asparagus ferns are rugged, sun-loving, healthy plants that are very easy to care for. All produce clouds of very fine foliage and, on occasion, white flowers with red berries. The three species I will discuss here are hardy to half-hardy and are quite easy to grow.

Asparagus ferns produce fleshy or even tuberous roots that can store some water. To grow them successfully, plant them in well-lit exposures in sandy soil. They can be fed frequently but require little other care.

Asparagus plumosus
Asparagus Fern

Asparagus plumosus comes in two forms. One is an upright twiner that can get 15 feet long and will crawl all over everything. The second form is var. nanus. It is the one we frequently see. It normally gets about 2 feet tall and is quite an upright plant. Both forms produce flat thin branches covered with needle-like foliage on the same plane, causing the entire affair to look as if someone ironed the branches flat. A. plumosus is the tenderest of the three and is probably best put near the house in an atrium or other protected areas where frost will not be as severe. It likes good drainage, water, food, good light and a trellis to climb on.

Asparagus retrofractus

Our second Asparagus, A. retrofractus, has only recently been introduced to the plant-growing scene. It is a delightful plant that forms a bush about 3 feet tall. Each branch looks like a soft green pom-pom, making the plant very distinctive. As with the other asparagus, it is easy to grow, likes sand, good light, some food, and drainage. Not a lot is known about its hardiness, but it appears to be hardy throughout our area, although the tops do get frozen back each winter.

Asparagus sprengeri
Sprengeri Fern

The most common and aggressive of the three species discussed is A. sprengeri. It is widely used in hanging baskets indoors and as a border outdoors. Normally it produces drooping fern-like masses of branches that go well in a hanging basket. It would, however, be superb along the top of a garden wall, on a slope near a waterfall, or wherever it is allowed to hang down.

The plant grows to about 3 feet in diameter in the garden, it produces white flowers in the summer and red berries each winter. It will grow in full sun, but looks better in some light shade where the foliage remains green instead of turning yellowish.

A splendid cultivar, called c.v. meyeri or the foxtail sprengeri, is very distinctive. Instead of cascading down, the meyeri form holds its branches erect to 24 inches, and creates a series of "fox-tail" branches. This form is rather new and somewhat more expensive than the common sprengeri, but it is just stunning in the garden. Consider the meyeri form as an accent plant to set off some corner of the garden.

(Left to right): Asparagus fern, Asparagus retrofractus, and Asparagus sprengeri.

Aspidistra elatior
Cast Iron Plant

Along with the Boston Fern, the cast iron plant is one of the old Victorian plants that has recently become very popular again. It has no stem, produces 18 inch leaves that are 6 inches wide and slowly taper to the leaf point and leaf base. This leaf, usually flopped over, pops out of the ground with no real purpose. The plant has no shape, produces no conspicuous flower and tends to maintain itself forever, which is why it is popular. It's tough to kill a cast iron plant, and that is why it has this name.

Cultivation is easy: any soil is fine; it will grow in dense shade or partial sun. It will stand all manner of neglect, and even our freezes.

If you need a hardy plant for a dark corner of the garden, this is it. If you do plant it, try to find a good variegated form. There are many variegated ones, but only a few are really pretty, so look for them.

Aucuba japonica
Gold Dust Plant

As indicated by the name, Aucuba japonica comes from Japan, not a tropical place. No matter, though—it is a great contribution to the tropical garden. It offers an upright bush to 4 feet, clothed in large evergreen gold-spotted leaves. It's flowers are negligible, but its bright foliage is a decided contribution the year-round.

Aucuba is completely hardy throughout our area. It does well in shade, wants to be kept damp, and enjoys a humus, acid soil.

There is also a dwarf form that is much more compact and would do well in tight areas where the full-sized plant might be too big.

Cast iron plant, a very tropical-looking yet cold-hardy plant.

Bambusaceae
Bamboos

For a group of plants as well known as the bamboos, it is surprising that they are not better represented in our gardens. Bamboos range from 6-inch dwarf groundcovers to towering giants over 100 feet tall. I suspect that a lack of understanding is the reason people don't use the plants more.

Bamboos are woody grasses and belong to the grass family. We generally think of bamboos as being native to the orient, but there are bamboo species in nearly all tropical areas, including North and South America. The group is generally believed to be tropical. There are, however, many species native to Korea and at least one species native to the United States. Some of these temperate species can withstand freezes to −30°F, and many species can withstand the worst of our Gulf Coast cold of 15° to 20°F.

Bamboos are of two types: running and clumping. The running type is the aggressive kind that sends out long underground runners in all directions. It is this type that scares some people because the bamboo plants can get very large if they are left uncontrolled. The second group, the clumping bamboos, form clumps that slowly get larger in diameter each year.

Bamboos are hot weather plants; the running types wait until late spring to start growing while the clumping types wait until August to grow. Once they begin, however, the new shoot can grow from 10 to 20 inches a day. Each new shoot reaches full size in a couple months, grows leaves, and does not get perceptibly larger ever again. If a bamboo plant wants to get taller, it grows a new shoot from the ground; it does not add height to an older shoot.

Bamboos uniformly like lots of moisture, water, and fertilizer. Running types are usually transplanted in late spring; clumping types in late summer.

Four interesting forms are included here to suggest the diversity possible with the bamboo family.

Arundinaria pygmaea
Pygmy Bamboo

Possibly the most dwarf of bamboos, this plant seldom gets even 1 foot tall. It has 4-inch green leaves and forms a dense mat. There is also a variegated form.

Bambusa glaucescens
Hedge Bamboo

This is one of the hardier bamboos. It forms clumps to 15 feet high and easily that wide. The yellow stems are about 1 inch or more in diameter. There is also a form with variegated leaves and stems, and a "fern-leaf" dwarf form.

Bambusa ventricosa
Buddha's Belly

In the garden Buddha's belly grows to about 50 feet, with dark green stems in clumps. In a large pot, however, it gets 8 feet tall and all the stem joints swell to form the "Buddha's belly" look. Don't over-feed in either case.

Sasa veitchii
Kuma Bamboo Grass

This is a rhizomatous form that stays quite low, usually under 1 foot high. It produces 8-inch-long leaves 2¼ inches wide. It is more ornamental than many of the other groundcover bamboos and is completely hardy.

(Left to right): Pygmy bamboo, striped stems of variegated hedge bamboo, and fully grown clump of Buddha's belly bamboo.

Leaf Textures

Giving your tropical garden real appeal very much depends upon the textured effects created by the plants you choose. Herb gardens and English border gardens have a variety of leaf colors to help accent the garden when it's out of flower. Tropical gardens, however, have an overwhelming greenness that pervades them, causing everything to blend together into a monotonous mass. You offset this by playing up the leaf textures, and certain plants can be used to create very appealing differentiations.

Bananas

Bananas, depending on the varieties used, can create two effects: overhanging droopiness (common banana) and a reaching erectness (Abyssinian banana). To be wholly successful with the big, droopy stance of the common banana, it is important to keep all the lower leaves completely trimmed off, thus accenting the yellow-green stems. The Abyssinian banana differs from other bananas since it holds its leaves starkly erect. The rigidly upright leaf form is very effective in giving the sensation of height.

Bamboos

Bamboos lend an erect air to the garden—that's why you want them, but most gardeners fail to realize that the smallest and oldest canes must be removed along with any lower secondary branches to achieve the classic bamboo feel.

Elephant Ears

Planted in masses in a well-lighted locale, elephant ears won't fail to provide a beautiful tropical effect. To fully attain this effect, it is important to keep the number of individuals down by removing many of the small suckers. You should also fertilize abundantly and remove any weak or older leaves.

Cyperus

The two forms of cyperus give unique and contrasting effects if properly displayed. Cyperus alterniflorus creates a startling effect with each parasol-capped stem, while C. papyrus creates gorgeous plumes on 10-foot stems that have great textural appeal.

Ferns

Most ferns get lost in the background, but two, Osmunda regina and O. cinnamomea, create an outstanding vase shape in shady areas. And tree ferns can totally dominate an entryway or other protected area with their soft foliage and unique trunks.

Palms

Certainly one of the most distinct groups are the palms. Among the most outstanding are the windmill palm, with its "burlap" covered stem, the cabbage palm with its curious overlapping leaf bases, the Australian fan palm, whose gray recurved fronds are very distinctive, and the short spreading Chinese fan palm which gets wider than it does taller.

Manihot

This decorative tropical creates a small round crowned tree in short order. Each palmate leaf is in itself very distinctive, and the collective effect is excellent.

Ricepaper Plant

Slower growing and more substantial than other tropicals, the huge leaves of the ricepaper plant are always useful in the garden, especially when a textured background is needed.

Selloum Philodendron

Widely seen and very distinctive, a well grown selloum remains a show stopper. Feed them well, give them room, keep the weak foliage removed, and let the plants work for you.

Plumeria

Accent plantings of a potted plumeria are very useful. The long barren stems topped with a head of leaves and flowers are a delightful contrast.

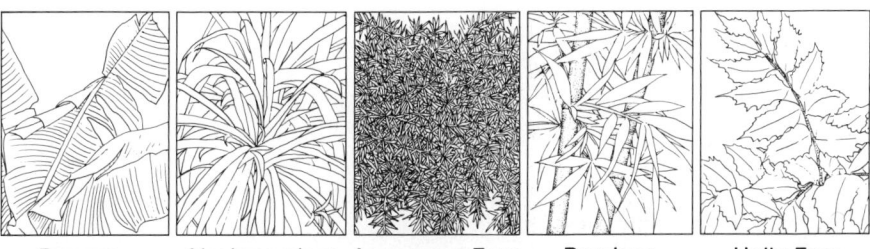

Banana   Airplane plant   Asparagus Fern   Bamboo   Holly Fern

Bauhinia sp.

Bauhinia is a gorgeous small tree with roundish leaves borne in pairs and large white or pinkish flowers to 4 inches across. The tree gets its botanical name from the double leaves which reminded some botanist of two French brothers, the Bauhins, both famous botanists. The derivation of the common names (below) is obvious: the exotic flowers remind many people of orchids.

As trees go, the bauhinia is rather sensitive. It does not like excessive cold, drought, or alkaline soil. To grow it successfully, you need an open, humus, acidic soil, even moisture, and protection during the winter. Since they are small trees, you can use them in large atriums or protected entryways. You might also consider an espalier of bauhinia along an east wall. In the southern parts of our area no protection is needed, but acid soil is always necessary.

Bauhinia corniculata
White Orchid Tree

This is the hardier of the two. It does well in sun or partial shade and produces its huge white flowers in late summer.

Bauhinia forficata
Orchid Tree

Another lovely tree, this one flowers in the spring. It is more tender than the other and comes in white or lavender. Another variety, Bauhinia purpurea, is similar but has purple flowers.

Beloperone guttata
Shrimp Plant

As the name implies the shrimp plant produces a flower cluster that is long, pink, segmented, and looks vaguely like a shrimp hanging off the plant. It is a robust plant that grows 3-4 feet tall and produces hundreds of flowers over the course of a year.

Beleperone is quite easy to grow. It needs the typical sandy loam soil, even moisture, partial shade, and protection from hard freezes. The plant is not hardy but will recover from moderate frosts by sprouting new stems from its roots. Hard freezes will kill it if no protection is afforded. So, mulch them in the fall, save cuttings for spring planting in a protected locale or cover the plants for hard freezes.

The shrimp plant is ideal for atriums and protected entrys. Since it is a smallish plant that is easily contained, it's just perfect in the small garden.

Clusters of shrimp plant flowers obscure the plant's leaves.

Bougainvillea sp.
Bougainvillea

As a source of color, the bougainvillea is one of the most flamboyant flowers of the tropical garden. Bougainvillea is the brilliantly colored vine that covers walls and cascades down cliffs throughout the tropics. The most popular forms are purple and red, but orange, pink, and white cultivars are coming on strong. There are even a double-flowered purple form and a highly ornamental variegated form.

All bougainvilleas get large. They will quickly climb 10 to 20 feet in all directions if allowed. On the other hand, a bougainvillea will flower well in a 10-inch pot. Throughout much of our region bougainvilleas freeze back severely in cold winters. Therefore, except in southern portions of zone 9, they should be treated as tub plants or otherwise carefully protected from hard freezes each winter.

Bougainvilleas are easy to grow, but they prefer a sandy, well-drained soil. Give them full sun, don't overwater, and trim back the rank growth. Bougainvilleas are notable additions to any tropical garden and everyone should try one, either potted or planted out.

Bromeliaceae
Bromeliads

Sometimes called the living vase plant, the bromeliad is a rosetti-form plant with stiff, colorful leaves that hold water in their bases and produce brilliant flowers of bright red, steel blue, canary yellow, etc. All bromeliads hail from the New World, and the family includes such diverse members as the pineapple and Spanish moss.

In general, bromeliads are colorful and very rugged, traits that endear them to indoor gardeners. It turns out that many bromeliads will survive a light frost (to 28°F), and a few are able to handle colder temperatures without much problem. Most bromeliads grow naturally in the trees. Of these, there are perhaps five or six species that can be established in our garden trees. A few others grow on the ground, and a couple of these can also be placed in the gardens. The hardy and semi-hardy bromeliads that can be grown in our area include the following groups:

diameter and 3 feet tall. It is completely hardy throughout most of our area, showing some damage only in the coldest of years. A word of warning: B. balansae is one of the best defended plants I know. Most cacti get jealous when they see a balansae. The plant's leaves are covered with hooked teeth that do not bend. In Mexico, the plant is effectively used as a fence. Also, the new shoots are edible and taste like water chestnuts; the only problem is collecting them. If you grow B. balansae, give it sun, room, and keep it out of traffic areas.

A gathering of bromeliads, one of the most diverse plant groups in nature.

Aechmea sp.

Many of the epiphytic aechmeas will take a limited frost of 30-32°F while A. calyculata appears to be hardy to 28°F. Aechmeas in general should be protected in a minimal manner; any protection that keeps them at or above freezing will get most through.

Billbergia nutans
Friendship Plant

Certainly one of the most common of bromeliads, this easily available member appears to be hardy to about 30°F. While B. nutans is a tree growing epiphyte, it can also be planted in the ground if the soil mix is very loose and well drained.

Bromelia balansae

This ground growing bromeliad looks like a huge pineapple plant and can form clumps up to 6 feet in

Neoregelia sp.
Fingernail Plant

The common name comes from the production of pink or red tips on the leaves at blooming time—some think these look like painted fingernails. Like the aechmeas, the neoregelias are semi-hardy to about 30-32°F, but a few will take 28°F without harm.

Tillandsia sp.
Ball Moss
Spanish Moss

These are by far the hardiest of bromeliads. The Spanish moss (T. usneoides) is native to all of the South and is completely hardy. To establish it, all you do is throw some clumps of it into any coarse-barked hardwood tree (like ash, oak or elm) and let it go.

T. recurvata and T. baileyi are, respectively, the small and giant ball moss bromeliads. Both are epiphytic and will grow in our area if wired to any hardwood. Both are native to various parts of the South, so they are completely hardy.

Brunfelsia calycina
Yesterday Today and Tomorrow

Aptly named, brunfelsia has small, round five-petalled flowers that open purple, turn bluish and fade quickly to white. The plant is a summer-blooming shrub that rarely gets over 4 feet tall.

Brunfelsia needs lots of moisture, partial shade and a loamy soil to succeed. The plant seems to be hardy throughout zone 9. It is especially useful in atriums and other small gardens where you want a plant that won't overpower its neighbors. The continually changing flower color fascinates the kids, so if you have children, grow one for them.

Butia capitata
Cocos Australis
Jelly Palm

Cocos Australis is possibly the most distinctive palm we can grow. It starts off with a heavy short trunk reminiscent of a date palm trunk. On top of this are long typical palm leaves that are blue-gray in color, curled outward and down. The plant looks like a huge pinwheel 10 feet high and wide.

Cocos Australis is one plant that really deserves center stage in the middle of the lawn. Set off by itself in a sunny location, the plant is just magnificent.

It is easily grown in an open, sandy soil. It needs full sun and should not be over-watered. Don't crowd it among other plants: it won't develop properly due to competition and shade. Give it a place of its own; it is worth it.

Cactaceae
Cacti

Cacti are not usually thought of as elements of the tropical garden, yet many cacti grow with orchids in trees in the tropics. Cacti also have some of the most delicate flowers imaginable. Besides, there's hardly a garden anywhere that doesn't have a dry, hot, sunny corner that would welcome a cactus but little else.

There are a great variety of cacti, and they have widely divergent requirements, yet all have a place in the tropical garden. Significant among these are the mission pear, various orchid cacti, and some cereus types.

Opuntia ficus-indica
Mission Pear

If you can imagine a plant composed of a bunch of oval pads 10 inches long, 8 inches wide and 1

Tillandsias, the most cold-hardy bromeliads.

inch thick, stuck end on end, you can imagine what the mission pear looks like. There are a number of varities of this plant, varying in stature and pad size, but all are spineless and have roughly the same habits and growth requirements.

Mission pears are completely hardy here. They prefer a bed of sand around the base, and full sun. Given proper light and the drainage the sand affords, the mission pear is hardy and ideal around lamp posts, in dry corners, along driveways and wherever else you need a carefree plant. To top off the whole delightful picture, mission pears bear delicious edible fruits that turn purple when ripe. Do be careful, though; there are small bristles all over the fruit, so peal it before you eat it.

Epiphyllum ackermannii
Orchid Cactus

This is one of mother nature's real jewels. Each spring, dozens of 4-inch orange flowers are produced on pendant flat stems about 2 feet long and 2 inches wide. The plant is tender and should be protected in a cool, dry place all winter. Also, with the pendant habit, the orchid cactus should be put in a basket in good light where it can develop to its fullest.

Cocos Australis, an excellent palm for the lawn.

Epiphyllum pumilum
Dwarf Orchid Cactus

This plant is similar to E. ackermannii but is much smaller in all respects. Pumilum produces tapered 8-inch stems that produce white 2-inch flowers. Like ackermannii, it needs a basket to do its best. It prefers a well-aerated sandy soil, water twice a week, good light, and winter protection. Big plants will reward the grower with hundreds of white flowers each year.

Epiphyllum strictum
Queen of the Night
Orchid Cactus

A third possibility for an orchid cactus is E. strictum. Unlike the other two, this plant grows upright. It produces 3-foot flat stems up to 3 inches wide. Given full sun, the plant will produce 80 to 100 6-inch white flowers each summer.

This epiphyllum blooms only at night; the other two remain open during the day. Like the others, it is easy to grow. It needs sun, a good sandy loam, water, but does not require a basket since it's branches are held upright.

Cereus peruvianus
Torch Cactus

One of the more common cacti, the torch cactus does well in areas where frost is not too severe. In these areas the cactus will quickly develop into a plant composed of several 4- or 5-angled blue stems with spines on the edges. At maturity, about 6 feet, the plant will produce many white 8-inch saucer-shaped flowers.

Like other cacti, it prefers sun and sandy soil. It will stand our rain if given drainage and protection from hard frost.

Trichocereus spachianus
Torch Cactus

This is another cactus that is relatively easy to grow. It produces many 3-foot branches in a clump that looks like an organ pipe, as well as huge white flowers each summer.

Like C. peruvianus, this will take some frost but needs protection from hard freezes. It also likes lots of sand and sun; otherwise it is quite easy to grow.

Flowers of the orchid cactus. In full sun, this plant can produce up to 100 of these flowers.

Caladium bicolor
Fancy-Leaved Caladiums

Caladiums are fancy-leaved tropical plants which are very popular outdoor plants in the South. Up north they are treated as houseplants. Caladiums come in a variety of garish colors, including white with green veins, red with dark red veins, green with red blotches, and a host of other pinks and combinations. All do well as borders along walkways and as colorful accents in shady nooks in the garden. They are especially appealing when planted around pools, where the water reflects the bright colors.

All caladiums are grown from bulbs planted in sandy loam, indoors, early in the spring. When the leaves get 8 inches tall, carefully transfer the bulbs to the garden, where they will grow profusely all summer if you provide them with plenty of moisture, fertilizer, and sandy humus soil. When fall approaches they will begin to die down as they go dormant. At this time the bulbs should be lifted, cleaned, and stored in a cool place for replanting next spring.

Caladiums can be planted in full sun or partial shade throughout the area. If you plant them in full sun, watch them carefully because they will stunt back if they get too dry. I prefer to place them in partial shade. In shady areas where they are protected from the wind, it is cooler, damper, and the leaves can grow larger with more color. In all, caladiums provide one of the most colorful additions to the tropical garden.

Caladiums, excellent plants for shady spots, are available in an array of striking colors.

Callistemon citrinus
Bottle Brush

The bottle brush tree (or shrub) comes to us from Australia, where it is a member of the large and unusual Protea family. In our area the bottle brush tree finds wide use as a hedge or foundation planting. It usually gets rather large, 10 feet high and 6 feet wide is common.

The shrub is evergreen and is covered with hard, narrow, plastic-like leaves. The flowers form along a section of newly developing branches; they are red, composed mostly of filament-like floral parts, and radiate in all directions about the branch, giving it the look of a brush.

Generally, bottle brushes are fairly hardy. They prefer sandy soil kept on the dry side, full sun, and some protection from excessive cold. The ones I've grown tended to die back a little each winter, but they quickly redeveloped their lost branches.

The common bottle brush gets somewhat unkempt if you don't prune it once in a while. Recently, a lovely compact, very floriferous form has been introduced, and it is worth looking for. There is also a dwarf form.

Canna indica
Cannas

Cannas are related to bananas and give a somewhat similar effect. They grow very well, are half-hardy throughout our area, and produce huge masses of foliage and abundant flowers. The plants establish easily and can actually become a problem since they are quite aggressive.

Cannas, as with nearly all the other plants here, like lots of light, food, and water. They are almost maintenance-free except for leaf-rolling caterpillars (about three kinds of them), which just love cannas. The cannas don't slow down because of the caterpillars; indeed, they keep right on growing very aggressively. However, the foliage will look pretty bad if you don't spray for these caterpillars. They are easy to control and usually don't show up until mid-summer.

There is a canna for every taste; from dwarfs of 2 feet tall to giants of 10 feet. They come in green or bronzy leaf and every color from yellow, pink, and bronzy brown to red and beyond.

The leaves and flower of the canna lily.

Carica papaya
Papaya

Papayas are famous as tropical fruits, but as garden plants they are hardly ever seen. Yet it is possible to grow them along the Gulf Coast, and in the more southerly parts of our zone they do rather well.

Papaya plants are usually single stemmed with huge lobed leaves sitting atop a 6-8-foot-long knobby green stem. Each papaya is either male or female, so it takes two to get fruit. As with many other fruiting tropicals (i.e., bananas), the effort involved in getting fruit in our area is probably not worth it. But the plants themselves are very distinctive.

In good years with reasonably warm winters, papayas will survive in protected areas. They will, of course, freeze back to the older wood and even to the ground, but usually they will redevelop in the spring. Given some protection, the plants will survive our winter very well.

Since it is doubtful that you will be able to consistently develop fruit on your papaya, consider searching out the "Flowering Papaya." This is a garden form that develops a profusion of larger, more colorful flowers than the typical plant. Papayas need an acid soil and moisture to avoid chlorosis or excessive leaf drop.

Papayas are another interesting plant to grow here along the Gulf Coast, as long as you don't mind losing one once in a while to an exceptional winter.

Carissa grandiflora
Natal Plum

The natal plum comes in a variety of sizes to accommodate a variety of uses. All forms are shrubby, with almost round, 1-inch, dark evergreen leaves borne in pairs that frequently overlap. Flowers are white with five long narrow petals, and later a purple plum often forms. The natal plum also produces small paired thorns all along the stem, so don't worry about kids messing around with the plant.

In northern sections of zone 9 the natal plum is sensitive to very hard freezes, but in southerly areas it is completely hardy.

The plant prefers a sunny, sandy locale, and not a whole lot of water. It is otherwise very easy to care for.

As mentioned, natal plums come in a number of shrubby forms. The standard shrub can get about 6 feet tall and 6 feet wide, but a whole variety of selected dwarf forms have been developed. There is a dwarf from up to 2 feet high, a very dwarf form

Symetrically segmented foliage of the papaya.

of a foot or so tall, and a super dwarf that is actually a ground cover of 8 to 10 inches tall. All of these forms spread around but are easily controlled. By virtue of the variation in size, natal plums find wide use as foundation plantings, groundcovers, along walkways, or wherever a short, spreading plant is needed in a sunny spot.

Casurina equisetifolia
Australian Pine

While it is not a pine, at least Casurina does come from Australia. The trees will reach 75 or more feet tall with a narrowish shape and peculiar, distinctive dusty green foliage that decidedly resembles the "horsetail rushes" you see along railroad tracks, etc.

Casurina seems indifferent to soils—but probably prefers some sand. It grows very large so keep it away from the house and sidewalks since its shallow roots will buckle cement walks, etc. In our area it does die back in a little in extremely harsh winters, but otherwise it seems to be quite hardy. The tree is very distinctive, so give some thought to it if you want a large and unusually textured tree for your yard.

Catalpa speciosa
Catalpa

Catalpas are huge native American trees that produce beautiful pink bell-shaped flowers each spring and long pods in the fall. The tree is canopied in heart-shaped leaves up to 12 inches long, giving it a very tropical look. Since it is native to our Midwest, the tree is completely hardy here. Trees in general have a decided lack of color in our area, but the catalpa's pink flowers offer a beautiful exception to this rule.

The tree is very easy to grow. It prefers a loam soil with moderate moisture all year round. Given this, the tree will grow about 4 feet in a good year to an ultimate height of 80 feet.

For small gardens, the huge size of a mature catalpa may be prohibitive. And some may find the long pods a nuisance. But to me, the catalpa is one of the most desirable of our native trees.

Ceratostigma plumbaginoides
Plumbago

Most people have a love-hate affair with plumbago. The plant is a lax-growing shrub that verges on the weedy side. It forms a mound of foliage 2 feet high and as wide as you allow it to go. Then along come the clusters of baby blue trumpet-shaped flowers that completely cover the bush. What a delight. The plants bloom nearly all summer and find wide applicability wherever a hardy small colorful bush is needed.

Plumbagos are hardy here but need to be trimmed severely early each spring. They do well in sun or partial shade and are indifferent to soil so long as it is well drained. They need even moisture all year. Simple care will provide you with a lovely bush of colorful flowers all summer.

Chamaerops humilis
Mediterranean Fan Palm

Here is another justly popular palm. The Mediterranean fan palm is one of our smaller clustering fan palms. Each head of fan-shaped leaves forms a mound about 4-6 feet wide. The plants usually cluster when young and these may be removed or left as you desire. There are occasional solitary plants, and these tend to be bigger individuals. Ultimately, the Mediterranean fan will get 10 or more feet tall, but it is a slow grower. The plant is often used as a foundation planting, but it is certainly pretty enough to be treated as a specimen planting as well.

This palm is completely hardy throughout our area. It seems indifferent to soils, but it probably appreciates a sandy loam most. Like many other palms it requires partial to full sun. Since it is a Mediterranean plant, it can get by on less water than many other plants. It doesn't even seem to be bothered by our occasional droughts.

Mediterranean fan palm.

Chlorophytum comosum
Variegated Airplane Plant
Variegated Spider Plant

Usually treated as an indoor or basket plant, the spider plant will do beautifully in the garden in sun or light shade. The plant is not the least bit temperamental about soil. They withstand rain and drought alike, but prefer a reasonably friable, well-drained soil if at all possible.

Spider plants are half-hardy in our area. They lose their foliage with the first frost but bounce back reliably each spring.

The variegated spider plant makes an attractive border plant. Its contrasting green and white leaves set off the pure green of other plants quite well. Trim off the "airplanes" (runners) occasionally if you want a more tidy-looking plant.

Cinnamonum camphora
Camphor Tree

As hinted at in the botanical name, the camphor tree is related to cinnamon. The tree itself is the source of camphor and camphor wood, used to make camphor chests, even the leaves smell of camphor when you crush them.

Camphor is not an American native; it comes from India. It's a delightful fast-growing evergreen shade tree that is pretty the year around. It develops a very broad dark green crown similar in some respects to our native live oak. It grows exceedingly fast and will withstand our winter's cold and occasional droughts without problems. I have never seen insects attack the tree, and it asks only to be watered occasionally when the ground is quite dry. In a good year the tree will add 3 to 5 feet in height and width. The plant is very undemanding, but responds aggressively to liberal fertilization and water.

Some people dislike its production of small berries, but I feel that problem is inconsequential. The camphor tree begins life as a shrub with several main trunks and branches to the ground. These lower branches and extra trunks can be pruned away to make a more typical looking tree, or perhaps three of the trunks can be left to add interest. Try to keep the lowest branches removed or they'll crowd out any other plants.

In all, the camphor tree is one of the most delightful trees available to the Gulf Coast gardener. Its elegant shape, evergreen nature, and few requirements should make it more popular than it currently is.

Citrus sp.
Orange
Lemon

Massive volumes are written on the Citrus family, its forms and culture. Those are for fruit growers. For the tropical gardener, citrus make a delightful addition to the garden by virtue of their lovely glossy green foliage, abundant and fragrant flowers, and the showy fruits produced by several varieties. There are also seemingly little-known variegated citrus varieties that are highly ornamental.

Since the various citrus range in size from dwarf shrubs to small trees, there are endless landscape possibilities for the enthusiastic gardener.

The general requirements for citrus include a sandy soil of neutral to acid pH, even moisture levels throughout the year, sun, and protection from severe frost. The only major problem with citrus is a scale insect. One frequently sees citrus foliage covered with black soot, which is a black mold growing on the juices exuded by the scale attacking the citrus. When you spray for the scale (usually in early spring), the black mold disappears because the scale no longer produces the exudate. Its not often that you can cure two ills with one spray!

In the fall certain caterpillars also attack citrus. These are usually quite ornate little creatures that move away from the tree during the daytime and return to forage at night. Not surprisingly, when you step on them they smell like citrus. Any general-purpose insecticide will control them, but avoid those insecticides with a systemic poison if you are going to eat the fruit. I won't attempt to cover all the possible citrus one could grow, I will confine myself to four that I consider reasonably ornamental and hardy enough to make it through our winters with a little protection.

Citrus limon
Ponderosa Lemon
Meyer Lemon

The lemon tree is very hardy and very large, often over 20 feet. There are, however, three interesting small forms.

The ponderosa lemon is a dwarf plant that produces pithy 2-pound lemons each of which is enough for a lemon meringue pie. It is grown more as a curiosity than anything else.

The rather similar, but smaller, Meyer lemon also produces a large fruit, up to ½ pound. It, too, is reputed to stay a short tree. Recently, I've seen a variegated lemon of unknown type. Like other variegated plants, it will doubtless be shy to flower or fruit, but it is quite ornamental.

Citrus mitis
Calamondin Orange
Miniature Orange

One frequently sees these for sale at supermarkets, in flower shops and garden shops. They are usually about 18 inches tall and have a dozen or

Calamondin oranges make interesting potted ornamentals for the house or patio.

more small round 1-inch oranges on them. In protected areas and in southern portions of our zone the calamondin is desirable as a dwarf shrub. It usually stays very short, less than 4 feet, very bushy and produces fantastic numbers of scented orange blossoms followed by sour oranges that are ideal for cocktails. There is also a delightful but somewhat more difficult variegated form available.

Citrus reticulata
Satsuma

This is one citrus that produces better fruit along the Gulf Coast than do the traditional commercial varieties. In the nursery the tree is grafted onto the trifoliate orange rootstock to produce a very productive, cold-tolerant dwarf tree which yields high-quality fruit. It will bear fruit in its second or third year and produce optimum quality fruit in its fourth. Besides, it has lovely fragrant flowers, and who can pass up the opportunity to brag to their northern friends "Well, we always grow our own oranges in the backyard."

Fortunella margarita
Nagami Kumquat

This citrus tree produces small oval kumquats which have a delicious peel and very bitter flesh. The tree is small and very productive. The fruit color is a beautiful bright orange, contrasting with the dark green foliage. Like the satsuma, it is grafted onto the trifoliate rootstock for maximum cold hardiness. Nagami kumquats make excellent yard trees, hedge rows, and container plants.

Codiaeum variegatum
Croton

Crotons are seen in gardens and landscapes throughout the world's wet tropicals. The reason is obvious: no plant has foliage more riotously colored than the croton's.

In time a croton will develop into an upright bush to 8 feet tall, covered with twisted or lobed garishly colored leaves of yellow, red, purple and green. There are an immense number of beautiful forms of crotons to grace the garden. The problem is deciding which ones to choose.

In the northern parts of our zone crotons need some protection from the cold; thus they are better treated as tub plants. These can then be kept out all summer and placed in a cool, frost-free room or garage during the winter. In the southern parts of zone 9 crotons are hardy and will reach immense sizes with little care.

Crotons should have the typical sandy loam with the slightly acid pH that most tropicals prefer. Don't let them dry out; keep them well fertilized and plant them in a sunny locale. Crotons need sun to develop proper coloration, so avoid shady plantings if you want intense color.

Coleus blumei
Coleus

Coleus is a beautiful ornate-leaved member of the mint family. It is always admired and is easy to grow. In our region coleus can be treated as an annual border plant. Cuttings placed out each spring will grow quickly into 2- to 3-foot-high mounds of foliage. Each fall, collect cuttings of your favorite forms and keep them through the winter for replanting next spring.

Attempts to keep coleus outdoors through the winter usually don't work well because the plants are tender; they freeze or rot, or both. With some care and protection, however you may be able to maintain them in the garden. Given an opportunity, coleus will develop into a sizable shrub of about 4 feet. By nature, coleus is not a bush, so it won't live long in the garden. It's better treated as an annual and replanted yearly.

Commelinaceae

This family comprises the wandering jew group, which includes a series of very similar plants in a variety of genera. Since they are all so similar, I have included them here. All wandering jews are groundcover type plants with ornamental leaves and small white or purple flowers. All do well in sun or shade; all prefer a rich soil, lots of fertilizer, and frequent watering. Wandering jews respond

The riotously colored foliage of the croton.

All About Elephant Ears

Elephant ears stand out as the most eye-catching and extraordinary plants in the tropical garden. There are many plants that have big leaves, but only a few have the requisite huge, spade-shaped leaf and fast growth that qualify them as bona fide "elephant ears." The most common, and to some the only, elephant ear is Colocasia esculenta, the taro. Two other plants, however, are sometimes confused with the taro and all three are treated together in this section.

Colocasia esculenta
Taro, the Common Elephant Ear

Taro, in addition to being a fine contribution to our tropical gardens, is also one of the most important food plants of the tropics. Throughout the South Pacific, taro is a food staple. No less than 50 varieties are cultivated around the world. One of these has even escaped in the southeastern United States and is now found in swampy areas from Louisiana to Florida.

The leaves of taro are shield-shaped, with smooth edges, and are held so the blade is facing outward and perpendicular to the ground. It is often not possible to determine which variety someone is growing unless the given plant is known to be growing under excellent conditions (only under ideal conditions will they develop fully, and ultimate size is the identifying factor).

Since most forms do not develop the huge leaves we want, it is best to begin your "herd" by purchasing a tuber of the "Giant" or "Common" elephant ear in the spring. Put this in a sunny area in rich soil, water it well, fertilize it abundantly, and stand back. A healthy taro will grow 6 feet tall and produce immense leaves 2 feet wide and 3 or more feet long. The plant can be considered half-hardy since it freezes to the ground each year but returns without fail the next spring. There is also a smaller form with purple blotched leaves.

Xanthosoma sagittifolium

Consistently confused with the taro, xanthosoma is more widely cultivated than people realize because they are always confusing it with the taro. Xanthosoma is separable from the taro by its more triangular leaves each of which has a vein running right along its edge. Xanthosoma also holds its leaves perpendicular to the stem so they are held upright rather than out like the taro's.

From what I can determine, there are no little-leaved or big-leaved forms of xanthosomas. Getting them big is just a matter of providing enough warmth, fertilizer, and water. In the garden this plant will get up to 6 feet tall with leaves 4 feet wide and 4 feet long. In protected areas they can get leaves 10 feet high, 6 feet wide and 6 feet long. Since the leaves are held upright, one can easily walk under them. There is a variegated form of this plant called the "pocket leaf" because of a deformity associated with the variegation.

(Left to right): Taro, the common elephant ear; Xanthosoma sagittifolium; and Alocasia macrorrhiza.

Alocasia macrorrhiza

The third, and for me the most interesting, elephant ear is alocasia. Unlike the others, this plant is rarely seen and grows quite slowly. When quite young the alocasia is difficult to tell from the taro, except that it has a wavy leaf margin and is greener. But at maturity there is no doubt about its identity. It produces leaves 6 to 8 feet high in a most peculiar manner. Unlike the others discussed, alocasia does not face its leaves out, so you can't see the shiny face. Rather, it holds them very erect so you see the backs of the leaves. The leaves themselves are lush green, spade-shaped, with prominent ribs and wavy margins. The blades are held straight up in the air and are parallel with the stems.

Like the other two elephant ears, alocasia freezes to the ground each winter and bounces back in the spring. It is a much slower grower than its associates. Give it time, space, food and warmth. There is a very distinctive variegated form of this plant also.

---

by producing lush aggressive growth about 8 inches tall that completely covers the ground. All forms freeze down each winter but return vigorously each spring. The only problem with them is that they are so aggressive they will crowd out other shorter plants.

I prefer to grow only one variety to a patch; a pure stand is more ornamental than a stand of mixed varieties.

Wandering jew also makes a hardy hanging basket. It will freeze, but the plants will regrow in the spring. There are a vast number of wandering jew types; four representatives are discussed here.

Callisia elegans
Striped Inch Plant

A more elegant jew than the others, this plant produces an emerald green leaf with narrow, white, parallel lines going from tip to base. The plant also produces white flowers each summer. It is especially nice in containers or on walls where it can cascade.

Setcreasea purpurea
Purple Heart

This form does very well as a short border or miniature hedge. It should be planted in full sun, where it will color up the most. I try to remove the older stems from the clumps so the younger erect ones are shown to advantage. This plant creeps more slowly than the others but produces a much bigger plant with 4-inch purple leaves and purple flowers.

Tradiscantia fluminensis
Green Wandering Jew

Possibly the most common of wandering jews, this is the small-leaved, all-green plant so commonly seen. It forms a thick mat if allowed and does well in the shade. There is a variegated form, too. Both forms eventually develop white flowers.

Zebrina pendula
Wandering Jew

This is another very common wandering jew. It produces silver and purple leaves with purple undersides. It is common in hanging baskets but also makes a stunning groundcover in sunny spots.

Cortaderia sellowiana
Pampas Grass

Pampas grass is not a plant for small gardens or protected entryways. It is for parking areas, near driveways or anyplace else a tough, drought-resistant large plant is needed. Pampas grass

Pampas grass: great for privacy, perfect for the pool.

forms a beautiful tall mound of grass with long flowing foliage and tall plumes each September. They can reach 6 feet tall and 8 feet wide. The grass is completely hardy here and has no particular requirements, except full sun, to develop properly. The leaves are minutely serrated, which can be a problem in traffic areas.

If you have room, they're great set off on the perimeters of a swimming pool. When it gets to mature size, pampas grass makes a nice screen for privacy while adding a "beachy" look to the pool area.

Cycas revoluta
Sago Palm

One of the old stand-bys of the Gulf Coast garden is Cycas revoluta, the sago palm. A member of one of the oldest plant families, the sago has been around for many millions of years. Somehow, I feel the plant knows about its heritage because it takes forever to grow!

The sagos come from Japan and China, where they are held in high regard. The plants resemble miniature palms, with stiff palm-like leaves coming out of a short trunk. Actually, the plant is not related to palms at all but is closer to pine trees, etc., with which it has in common the production of seeds in cones instead of from flowers.

Sagos are very popular because they are so hardy and they don't take over the garden like so many other tropicals. They are usually expensive since they grow so slowly. A typical sago will grow one set of leaves a year and add only 1 or 2 inches of stem height each season.

The plants produce huge fleshy roots and prefer sandy soil in full sun with lots of water. Shade causes them to get ungainly, so put them in bright places.

Cynara scolymus
Artichoke

Artichokes are members of the thistle family usually grown for their flower buds that are boiled and eaten with spiced butter. But artichokes make stunning foliage plants. The coarse-leaved plants are often seen in the foggy regions near San Franciso. Here in our Gulf Coast the huge gray feathery plants will form massive clumps to 6 feet in diameter and 5 feet tall, providing certain qualifications are met.

It seems that artichokes love our foggy, damp falls and springs, and they'll survive our winters without problems. However, getting them through July and August can be a task—they do not like

Sago palm, a very hardy and manageable palm.

heat. My suggestion is to plant them in a partially shady area under a deciduous shade tree that will allow light to get through. Another possibility is to plant them on the east side of the house. There the plants get an abundance of morning sun but miss the hot afternoon heat that is so detrimental. Artichokes must have an open, sandy soil, with lots of food and moisture. And if your area gets a lot of fog, and has sandy soil, they will do very well.

Cyperus sp.

The genus Cyperus is composed of a large number of grass-like plants that are usually found in swamps, along rivers, and in other wet places. Two very distinctive members of the genus, C. alternifolia and C. papyrus, are seen in Gulf Coast gardens. Both have the highly desirable talent of growing in wet soil. They prefer it, actually. And both also prefer full sun to partial shade and lots of fertilizer. These two plants provide some of the most distinctive shapes in the tropical garden.

Cyperus alternifolia
Umbrella Plant

By far one of the most popular tropicals along the Gulf Coast, the umbrella plant is a mainstay of the tropical garden. It works well as a screen, along walks, near traffic areas or wherever you need a plant that is tolerant of abuse.

Each umbrella plant grows about 4-5 feet tall and is composed of a series of green canes with 8-inch flat, narrow leaves radiating in every direction, forming the "umbrella." The plant is grown from divisions of the crown planted in the spring. It likes water, light, and fertilizer; given these the plant will grow explosively.

In winter a hard freeze will kill it back, but it quickly regenerates its top the following spring. It is an effortless plant throughout our zone.

Stylized lines of the umbrella plant.

Cyperus papyrus
Egyptian Paper Plant

Here is a plant steeped in history. Years ago (about 3,000), the Egyptians used to split the round canes of this plant in half, place the cut surfaces crosswise on one another, and then beat the stems flat to make writing parchment. It was on the pulp of this plant that much of civilization's first records were kept.

It's interesting that such an important ancient plant now is in vogue as a highly fashionable and artistic landscaping accent to the ultra-modern house.

C. papyrus produces 8- to 10-foot high, round canes that are topped with a "puff" of fine branch like leaves. The plant looks like something from the moon, only it's green. The very stylized lines are useful in a variety of places, and designers have fallen in love with them.

The Egyptian paper plant is easily grown in a pot of rich soil, standing in water. It requires sun to develop fully; otherwise it is easy to grow. In northern parts of our zone it needs protection from frost each winter. In southern parts the plant will do very well outdoors as long as it gets enough water and food.

For those who find the full-sized plant overwhelmingly large, there is a dwarf form that gets about 2 feet tall, but it is not as ornamental.

Cyrtomium falcatum
Holly Fern

The holly fern grows wild in the warm temperate forests of China. The plant produces coarse dark green fronds that are particularly desirable because they are evergreen and don't die down each winter. It forms small rosettes of foliage about 18 inches in diameter and a foot tall.

Holly ferns are among the hardiest of ferns, able to withstand our heat, cold, and occasional dryness without much complaint. The plants like an open humus soil in the shade. They also appreciate being kept damp, though they are not as demanding in this regard as other ferns are.

Holly fern.

Dicksonia antarctica
Tasmanian Tree Fern

Tree ferns are a problem in the northern parts of zone 9 because it gets too cold for them. The one delightful exception to this is the Tasmanian tree fern, which is allegedly able to withstand temperatures of 10°F. I worry about that claim, but this plant will doubtless withstand temperatures of 25° or less for short periods.

With this margin, the Tasmanian tree fern should find wide use in protected entryways, etc., where its smaller size can be appreciated. Other tree ferns can get up to 30 feet tall and 10 feet wide; the Tasmanian tree fern is much more manageable, with a trunk up to 6 feet and a leaf spread of about 4 feet. The plant thus has great utility near entryways, pools, in patios, and anywhere else the simple requirements of shade, loose acidic soil, and constant moisture can be met.

Dioon edule
Dioon

This is a Mexican cycad similar to Cycas revoluta but has a duller-colored leaf that is flatter and larger. Dioon forms a rosette of somewhat spiny leaves about 4 or 5 feet in diameter; like the cycas, it is very slow to grow.

Dioon can be grown in sun or partial shade. It needs even moisture and a rich soil but does not want to be over-fertilized. It appears to be completely hardy, but in northern areas protection in hard freezes will prevent damage to the beautiful leaves.

Use dioon as a specimen planting in atriums, near walkways, or wherever a distinctive plant is desired. It will never take over nor will it get too large.

Dioscorea sp.

From the genus Dioscorea comes the edible yam, widely cultivated as an important food crop. In our gardens the Dioscorea genus provides us with a highly ornamental vine which can be used as a quick cover or twiner in a variety of garden locations. Two members of the yam family are cultivated in southern gardens, both are distinctive, hardy, and highly ornamental.

Dioscorea bulbifera
Air Potato

Here is another vine for the incurable romantic. The air potato produces a large vine each season that is covered with heart shaped leaves up to 10 inches in diameter. It will grow 30 to 50 feet if given lots of food, but it dies completely to the ground each fall.

The plant produces thousands of minute flowers that are absolutely unnoticeable; its main attraction is its heart-shaped foliage and its production of aerial tubers—"air potatoes." About mid-season the plant will begin to develop brown potatoes all along its stem. These potatoes will vary from marble-sized midgets to potatoes 6 inches long, weighing ½ pound. Each of these can be planted the following spring to produce its own new vine. Underground, the potato will continue to grow until it is bigger than a bowling ball and almost as heavy. Don't try to eat the potatoes, though—they are very bitter.

Since the plant has a tuberous root, it should be planted in a sandy soil, or else it will rot. Beyond the necessity for sand around the tuber, little else is required. Air potatoes grow in sun or shade and prefer lots of food to grow best.

Dioon, slightly larger than the Sago palm, has showy leaves that create a focal point in the garden.

Heart-shaped foliage of the air potato vine.

Dioscorea macrostachya
Elephant's Foot

Elephant's foot plants are a big import from Mexico these days. They are usually cultivated for their huge tortoise shell-like tuber that sits on the surface of the ground. Like the air potato, it produces heart-shaped leaves on a vine, but these are only about 4 inches long.

If you want to cultivate the elephant's foot, it is best placed in a shallow pot or in a drier section of the garden where the bulb won't rot. Also, since the bulb is the attraction, place it in a location where you can see it.

The elephant's foot is reasonably hardy here. In mild winters even the leaves won't die down. The only requirement is keeping the tuber on sandy, well drained soil. The vine will grow in sun or shade and provides a smaller, more manageable version of the air potato vine.

Smaller, more elongate leaves of the elephant's foot vine.

Eriobotrya japonica
Loquat

Loquats are large ornamental bushes with wrinkled evergreen grayish leaves and fragrant fall flowers, followed by edible orange fruit. The bush grows up to 10 feet tall and wide. It is ideal as a specimen shrub, foundation shrub or background plant.

The loquat is completely hardy throughout zone 9 and is very popular in gardens here because of its evergreen nature, unusual foliage, fall flowers and fruit, and ease of culture.

Loquats prefer an open, sandy acidic soil, even moisture, and partial shade to full sun.

Erythrina crista-galli
Coral Bush
Coral Tree

This is the most distinctive bush in the South. It produces trifoliate leaves in clusters (like clover); its branches are long and have thorns on them, giving the bush a "swept up" appearance. But the real attraction is the huge red sweetpea-like flowers that grow in long bunches on the ends of each big branch. These unusual flowers are produced all summer on a bush that slowly gets up to 8 feet high and wide.

The coral bush is not dependably hardy in northern parts of zone 9. It freezes back severely in hard winters in any unprotected areas. But in southern parts of our zone it is quite hardy. Other requirements include lots of sun, open sandy soil, and care to avoid overwatering.

Eucalyptus sp.
Gum Tree
Eucalyptus

Most eucalyptus hail from Australia, where several hundred species exist. In the United States they are planted in mild climates because they are usually quite sensitive to frost. Along our Gulf Coast we grow a few eucalyptus that can with-

The ornamental loquat. This tree produces edible fruit and lovely flowers in the fall.

stand some frost. Generally, they are short-lived here because of weather and soil conditions, but if you are looking for a most curious tree, eucalyptus is it.

Eucalyptus are silver-leaved trees that tend to be very tall and narrow. Most eucalyptus shed their bark, which makes them even more strange.

Eucalyptus, especially young ones, prefer a sandy open soil with even moisture, lots of sun, and protection from frost. They seem to get hardier as they get older. One of the more interesting, and hardy, ones is the following species.

Eucalyptus pulverulenta
Silver Dollar Eucalyptus

This very distinctive plant has disc-like silver leaves with a stem going right through. You've seen them in some of the far out floral arrangements. The "silver dollars" only form on young trees. As they get older the fused younger leaves separate into two oblong silver leaves.

This plant freezes back in cold years, but if you treat it as a shrub it should do quite well.

Euphorbia pulcherrima
Poinsettia

The very popular Christmastime flower is a wonderful addition to the garden. Planted out in protected areas or near foundations of houses, the poinsettia will develop into a magnificient 8-foot-high rounded shrub with 15-inch flowers on each branch. The flowers normally develop around Christmas, so they provide a delightful source of late fall color. Poinsettias come in a variety of colors, including several reds, a pink, a white, a white with green in it, and other variations.

Cultivation of poinsettias is more complicated than some other tropicals. Plant them in a warm sunny place where frost will not hit them until after Christmas; or, you can provide them with some protection near and during flowering. Put the plants out in spring and let them establish. Fertilize them heavily, and be sure to keep them damp but not wet.

Prune them occasionally to develop a bush shape. Continue the occasional pruning until early August. After this, let them continue to grow and feed them well, but don't prune them any longer. Now is when the large flowering branches are forming.

As they grow, some branches may need to be staked. About October you will notice the plant has stopped growing and a bud is starting to form along with the colored brackets. From October until Christmas you don't have to do anything except protect them from frost. After Christmas, in late winter, cut the plants all down to a foot or two from the ground and start the process over again.

In southern parts of zone 9 poinsettias will not need protection, but in the northern parts and in unprotected areas they will need some frost protection to bloom well. Don't plant poinsettias near outdoor lamps or street lights. They are short-day plants and the light all night will cause them to flower improperly.

Poinsettias, the "Christmas plants," add a welcome splash of color when they bloom late in the fall.

Eucalyptus cinerea, a lovely ornamental tree for the Gulf Coast area.

Fatsia japonica
Fatsia

Here is another Japanese plant commonly thought of as a tropical. Fatsia is related to aralia and English ivy; in fact, there is an interesting hybrid of fatsia and ivy (Hedera) called Fatshedera, the tree ivy. The hybrid is intermediate between the two parents. Fatsia itself is a moderate-sized shrub with evergreen palmate leaves about 8 inches across and inconspicuous flowers. The plant slowly develops into a shrub 4 feet or larger.

Fatsia is hardy here and does well either in full shade or partial sun. Don't put it in full sun. It prefers the cooler, damper conditions that shade provides, and full sun will burn the leaves. Fatsia is useful in a variety of shady locations like atriums, northern exposures, under trees, etc.

Ficus sp.
Fig

The genus Ficus contains such diverse species as the common rubber plant (Ficus decora), the true fig (Ficus carica), the Banyan tree (Ficus Benghalensis), and even the viny creeping fig (Ficus pumila). The entire genus is tropical in nature, but several members will grow successfully in our area. All are easy to grow in average soil, and all like water, warmth, humidity, and good light. All can be propagated by air-layering, and some spontaneously produce aerial roots, making cuttings a simple matter. Three species of figs can easily be grown in our area. Two are completely hardy here, the third is half-hardy.

Ficus carica
Edible Fig

The edible fig is quite hardy throughout our area. It forms a deciduous bush or small tree to about 15 feet in all dimensions. Several varieties of edible fig are available; all produce well but it's best to choose the variety recommended for your area since some varieties are less tolerant of local rainfall and soil conditions than others (check with your county horticulturist).

The handsome foliage of Fatsia japonica, the Japanese aralia. This evergreen likes to be slightly cool, but it likes light, too. Place in filtered light/shade for an effective compromise.

Ficus decora
Rubber Tree

F. decora is well known as a decorative houseplant. In the more northerly and exposed areas of the Gulf Coast, F. decora is half-hardy, dying to the ground each winter and redeveloping each spring. In the southerly portions of our zone the common rubber plant will form a spreading 20-foot tree.

Many forms of this plant are available. In addition to the common green form, there are burgundy-leaved, small-leaved, and narrow-leaved forms and at least three distinctive variegated forms. The variegated forms should be well protected, as they are not as hardy as the all-green. The common rubber plant is ideal for protected entryways and near buildings, etc.

Ficus pumila
Creeping Fig

The creeping fig makes an ideal, hardy wall cover. It climbs via small roots produced along the stem and bears 1-inch, oval, evergreen leaves. It will grow on almost any wall but does best on the cooler, damper east and north walls. Given some food and water, the vine will cover a wall with evergreen leaves in just a few years.

Firmiana simplex
Chinese Parasol Tree
Japanese Varnish Tree

The Chinese parasol tree is one of many quick-growing trees for the tropical garden. It forms an upright 30-foot deciduous tree with lobed leaves 8 inches wide, and produces pretty ½-inch yellow flowers. The bark on the Chinese parasol tree is a prominent light green, unlike the common brownish bark of most trees.

The tree is hardy all over our area and is tolerant of our soils, heat, etc. It is an easily managed tree with a unique form and appearance.

Gardenia jasminoides
Gardenia

Gardenias are evergreen shrubs that eventually grow to 8 feet or more in diameter and bear vast numbers of pure white, intensely fragrant flowers each spring. The shrub is ornamental both in and out of flower and is a popular landscape plant everywhere along the Gulf Coast.

To successfully grow gardenias, you must provide moisture and acid soil. Any seasonal lack

Ficus decora, the rubber tree.

of moisture will kill gardenias, while alkaline soils cause all the leaves to turn yellow and drop off. So, provide good light and a very acid, humus soil. Keep the soil moist, and spray occasionally to keep the white flies and spider mites at bay during the hot months of July, August, and September.

In addition to the common gardenia, there are a dwarf form and a recently introduced yellow variety.

Gerbera jamesoni
Transvaal Daisy

Gerberas add a dashing bit of color to any tropical garden. Their daisy-like flowers are brilliant white, pink, yellow or red. Flowers are borne all summer from the small plants' ruffled foliage. They're just right for beds and work especially well in borders or elsewhere a bright spot of color is needed.

Gerberas do well in full sun to partial shade. They need an open loamy soil and continuous moisture to flower well. They'll freeze down in hard winters, but a loose dry mulch or similar covering will bring them through.

Graptopetalum paraguayense
Hen and Chicken
Dusky Rose

The dusky rose is a very hardy member of the jade family. It is often planted in flower beds, along walkways, and as a groundcover in hot, dry sunny places. Dusky rose also works wonderfully as a hanging basket plant in sunny locations, and you don't really have to remember to water them.

Dusky rose is comprised of a 3-inch rosette of fleshy, silken gray leaves produced on a weak stem. The plant trails along the ground, quickly forming colonies by branching or sprouting new plants from fallen leaves.

Of all plants, this must be the easiest to grow. But it does have its preferences: sandy soil, full sun, and occasional water. If you provide it with sandy soil and good drainage, it will grow without fail anywhere in our area, and out-of-doors it will never need water.

Hedera helix
English Ivy

One could make an entire collection of nothing but varieties of English ivy. Ivy, of course, needs no introduction. You see it everywhere as a ground and wall cover. The Hallowed Halls of Ivy would be barren without it.

English ivy is not a tropical plant: it comes from the Baltic region of Europe and is completely hardy everywhere in zone 9. And since it is so hardy here, we can plant the more interesting forms which would freeze in gardens further north. Instead of planting plain old English ivy, consider glacier ivy, a variegated version that comes in several forms. There is also "needlepoint" ivy, which has very intricate dwarf leaves. For the incurable romantic there is even a heart-shaped ivy that is completely hardy. Imagine, a whole wall of green hearts!

All these ivies prefer shade, water, and some support if they are to climb; otherwise they will trail across the ground to the exclusion of all else. They do not like *full* sun in our area, but they enjoy a splash of sunshine in the mornings.

Hedera canariensis
Algerian Ivy

This ivy resembles English ivy except that its leaves are larger, and lobed rather than pointed. The leaves are not as ornate as English, but the plant is easy to grow even in sunny areas, and it is quite aggressive. Algerian ivy tolerates more sun than English ivy, but it also needs more moisture.

Hedychium coronarium
Butterfly Ginger

This is the hardiest and most commonly seen ginger in coastal tropical gardens. It forms clumps of two-ranked leafy stems up to 6 feet tall. Each of these is topped by a cluster of white, fragrant "butterfly" flowers that last several days.

The plant requires lots of food, sun, warmth, and moisture to do well. It especially resents being disturbed. Each time you move one you can expect to

Hanging basket of English ivy.

Flowering butterfly ginger.

wait two or more years for them to decide to flower again.

Butterfly gingers are not too interesting out of flower, so keep them toward the back of the garden where they can grow tall and show off their flowers when in bloom and remain inconspicuous when they're not blooming.

Heliconia sp.
Heliconia

Heliconias are superb, exotic members of the banana family. In Hawaii and other tropical areas they are used as hedge plants or specimens for their exotic flowers.

The heliconia is fashioned like a small banana tree. It has wide-bladed leaves 10 inches across and 2 feet long, borne on long thin petioles. Each plant gets up to 6 feet tall, has a few leaves, and clusters profusely.

Flowers are the real attraction of heliconias. The flowers are similar to those of the bird of paradise, only more intricate and colorful. Depending on variety, they are bold yellow, orange, red or blue streaked, held strictly upright or hanging down from the top of the plant to the ground.

Along the Gulf Coast most heliconias are tender; they do not like our winter cold, so some precaution must be made for frost in all but the most southerly parts of zone 9. They are best treated as tub plants, put in humus soil with lots of sand or perlite, fed frequently, and given lots of warmth and light. In the winter when the plants are down, keep them dry until new growth appears.

If you're an adventurous gardener you can plant them out in a protected spot, but be prepared to give them cover and some warmth whenever frost is anticipated.

Three of the most dramatic heliconias are H. angustifolia, H. humilis, and H. rostrata.

Heliconia angustifolia

This heliconia comes from Brazil, grows to about 3 feet tall, and produces an upright flower composed of six or more green to red bracts and white petals with red bases.

Heliconia humilis

H. humilis grows up to 6 feet tall and has salmon-red bracts that are edged with chartreuse.

Heliconia rostrata

Another 4- to 6-foot plant, H. rostrata bears hanging clusters of flowers with red-tipped yellow bracts and yellow flowers. It is perfectly stunning.

Hibiscus rosa-sinensis
Hibiscus

A tropical garden without a hibiscus is like a zoo without animals. Hibiscus are those garishly colored, trumpet-shaped five-petaled flowers you see in every exotic travel folder. They form lovely 6-foot evergreen shrubs that continually produce flowers all year. They come in a variety of flashy colors, including red, yellow, orange, white, and pink and recent hybrids are producing flowers up to 8 inches across!

Hibiscus is tender in much of zone 9. For this reason they are treated either as tub plants or as shrubby annuals. If you treat them as tub plants, give them room, water, sun, food and fertilizer, and move them in during freezing weather. If you treat them as annuals, they can be handled like copper plants (see page 33).

Hibiscus flower.

In the spring, purchase rooted cuttings of your favorite color. Place these in the garden in an open, rich soil, in partial shade to full sun. Keep them damp and well fed. They will grow explosively all summer and bloom profusely on the newly developed branches. In fall, let them freeze or take cuttings to hold over for next spring. Then you start the process over again.

In protected and southern areas of zone 9, hibiscus can be kept out all year. You need only feed them well and give them lots of sun and water.

One problem is that hibiscus flowers only last a day (some new hybrids last up to three days). No matter—the hibiscus is always able to produce more flowers each new day.

Hippeastrum striatum
Amaryllis

The amaryllis is the Cadillac of flowering bulbs, producing four to five 8-inch trumpet-shaped flowers per stem for a couple of weeks each spring. These flowers come in brilliant red, white, pink, pink and white striped, red and white striped and too many more to list. After its spectacular floral display, the plant settles back to producing lance-shaped leaves 2 feet long and 2 inches wide. When the flowers are spent, pinch them off to prevent the formation of seed pods.

Amaryllis is completely hardy, dying back to a huge bulb each fall and producing flowers and new leaves the next spring. They will grow in full sun or partial shade, in a loose, sandy humus soil.

Amaryllis cannot be overfed. In fact, to bloom properly they require high levels of bulb food (a mixture of bonemeal and superphosphate works well) throughout their growing season. You do not want them to run short of water either, or you will induce dormancy before the plants are ready.

The name amaryllis is also applied to the true amaryllis (A. hallii), also called the mystery lily because it blooms in the fall without leaves. It, too, is hardy here and does quite well, but watch out for confusion over the names.

Hymenocallis sp.
Spider Lily

The spider lily is one of the largest and most exotic lily-type plants available for the southern tropical garden. The plant produces many 3-foot narrow green leaves about 3 inches wide. Out of these develop long 3-foot stems of fragrant, white trumpet-shaped flowers, with long narrow petals radiating out from the trumpets.

Cultivation is simple: the plant likes a very damp soil with lots of fertilizer and sun. That's about it. Spider lily is completely hardy in the Gulf Coast area.

Spider lily.

Variegation: Shades of Another Color

The tropical garden by its very nature is predominantly green. Tropical plants generally bloom in a rather haphazard way, flowering when they get the compulsion with little regard for the season. One way to resolve the green domination is with the addition of variegated plants whose foliage offers a pleasing contrast of color and design to the garden.

Variegation takes many forms. Leaves may be dotted, spotted, blotched or mottled. They may be bold-striped or bordered; however the variegation presents itself, it nearly always enhances the plants' appeal. The variegation actually is a result of the plants producing areas of cells in each leaf that do not have any chlorophyll. Without chlorophyll, the cells' undertone colors are free to show through as white or yellow variegation.

Variegation is occasionally caused by a virus. If a plant *suddenly* develops a variegated pattern and it spreads through the plant, it is probably diseased. Virtually all those plants that are sold as variegated are healthy, however, so don't worry about it unless you suspect something really is wrong.

Virtually every plant species has an individual that is variegated; the problem is to find it. Some variegated forms command a great deal of money, especially variegated palms and cycads. Others are very common, such as variegated spider plants or variegated pittosporum. Because of the obviously esthetic nature of most variegated plants, lately a great deal of interest has developed in them.

Variegated plants tend to be smaller, weaker, slower to grow and flower, and are usually less hardy than their all-green cousins. The reason for this is simple: when a plant produces a full-sized leaf, it only gets a return on its investment from the all-green portion of that leaf. The white or yellow portions do not contribute anything. In fact, the plant must support the variegated portions. This causes an extra energy drain, and that affects the growth potential of the plant.

But, beyond all this, variegated plants are beautiful and are worthy of any extra effort needed to keep them healthy. They contribute much needed color to the garden. Frequently, the leaf patterns are highly decorative. With some care it is easy to pick up many variegated plants that are hardy, easy to grow, and contribute immensely to the garden.

There are thousands of variegated varieties of plants. Some plants, like the common rubber plants, have several variegated forms, others just one form. The following list is presented as an inducement to your thinking. It is not complete, but it will give you an idea of the kinds of variegated plants available and those that you might want to consider for your tropical garden.

Acuba japonica	Gold Dust Plant	Hedra helix	Glacier Ivy
Agave americana	Century Plant	Heliconia sp.	Heliconia
Alocasia macrorrhiza	Elephant Ear	Liriope sp.	Liriope
Alpinia sp.	Ginger	Monstera deliciosa	Split-Leaf Philodendron
Aspidistra sp.	Cast Iron Plant	Nerium oleander	Oleander
Bougainvillea	Bougainvillea	Phormium tenax	New Zealand Flax
Caladium bicolor	Caladium	Pothos scandens	Pothos
Callisia elegans	Inch Plant	Rhoeo discolor	Moses in a Boat
Chlorophyllum comosum	Spider Plant	Sultana impatiens	Sultana
Citrus limon	Lemon	Syngonium podophyllum	Nephthytis
Codiaeum variegatum	Croton	Trachelospermum jasminoides	Confederate Jasmine
Coleus blumei	Coleus		
Ficus decora	Rubber Plant	Tradiscartia fluioninalis	Wandering Jew

Variegated specimens (from left to right): crotons, Xanthosoma (elephant's ear), glacier ivy (variegated English ivy), and manihot (variegated manihot esculenta).

Impatiens sultani
Sultana
Impatiens

Sultana is a very popular flowering houseplant up north; here in the South we can use this delightful shade-loving plant outdoors. It forms a bush about 15 inches tall which is covered with flat five-petaled flowers of white, pink, orange, red, purple or spotted. There is also a form with variegated leaves.

Sultanas grow well from seed or from cuttings rooted in water. They should be planted in partial to full shade where it is cool and damp. Sultanas have a problem with our summer heat, but planting in the shade alleviates this. The flowers are especially bright in spring and fall, when the weather is cooler and more damp.

Sultanas are not frost-hardy here, but you have three options for preserving them: cover or plant in a protected place; take cuttings in the fall and keep them through the winter for spring replantings (this is quite easy because they root quickly and like the dimmer light conditions on a window sill); or let them seed and sprout on their own. Sultana seed overwinters well and sprouts at the right time in the spring. The only drawbacks are that the plants don't always sprout where you want them and the seed of hybrid forms doesn't always replicate the parent plants.

Impatiens sultani, a plant that will grow and flower best in the shade.

Jacobinia carea
Jacobinia

Of the many tropicals discussed in this book, jacobinia is one of my real favorites. A properly grown jacobinia will produce a lovely shrub about 4 feet tall and 3 feet wide, covered with dark green leaves and, several times each season, topped with mounds of pink flowers.

Jacobinia carea is half-hardy in our area, dying down in the winter and redeveloping from its roots the next spring. It prefers partial shade—too much sun causes the foliage to yellow severely. This is a quick grower and, to support this habit, it needs ample fertilizer.

Jacobinia can be successfully propagated from woody cuttings taken just after flowering. The plant is a bit sensitive to disturbances, so be careful about moving it. Also, it is very brittle, so avoid putting it in traffic areas.

Mounds of jacobinia flowers.

Koelreuteria bipinnata
Golden Rain Tree

The golden rain tree is not exactly tropical in nature, since it comes from temperate climates, but it certainly looks tropical with its huge compound leaves, clouds of yellow flowers in midsummer, and inflated pink Chinese lantern-like seed pods each fall. (Another golden rain tree species, K. paniculata, is more cold-hardy than K. bipinnata, but its seed pods are a less spectacular brown color.)

This tree is one of the best small trees southerners can buy. It grows up to 30 feet tall, producing a round crown of large double-compound leaves. And it is very hardy and quick-growing: in its first few years a golden rain tree will add 4 to 6 feet a year in height and breadth

The plant is particularly desirable because it remains reasonably short, establishes well, blooms in an otherwise dull time of the year, and is seldom bothered by pests.

If you are willing to provide a well-drained soil, sun, and heavy fertilization, the golden rain tree will never fail to produce its lovely summer flowers.

Lagerstroemia indica
Crapemyrtle

Crapemyrtle, perhaps the prettiest of shrubs (or trees), is widely planted in the South and is a warm-temperate species, so one might argue that it has no place in the tropical garden. But the plant has such a vigorous habit, such brilliant colors, and such exotic floral shapes that I feel it's a must.

Crapemyrtles, of course, are the large shrub/trees we so frequently see canopied in large terminal clusters of white, red, pink or purple ruffled flowers much of the summer. They are large plants, growing to 15 feet tall and 10 feet wide with ease.

Crapemyrtles are completely hardy throughout our zone. Indeed, they need a winter rest to flower properly. They also need full sun, rich well drained soil, and abundant food to encourage flowering.

Each spring they need a severe pruning to remove all the weak branches and shorten the strong ones. Crapemyrtles bloom on new wood. The healthier and larger the new wood is, the more flowers will be produced. So, prune and feed them well.

If the size of the normal crapemyrtle is too large, look for the dwarf forms. These are just as pretty and they only get about 3 to 4 feet tall.

Another variety, L. faurieri, the Japanese crapemyrtle, has a vase shape, small white flowers, cinnamon-red bark and a more pointed, oriental appearance.

Lantana camara
Lantana

Lantanas are small hardy shrubs that bloom profusely and grow aggressively. Normally, they form bushy mounds 1 to 3 feet high and 4 feet wide. They come in all sorts of colors: white, pink, purple, yellow, orange, etc. The flowers of the lantana have different colors as the plant gets older, so groups of flowers on the same plant may be in several colors.

The crapemyrtle is one of the loveliest shrubs you can plant. Clip off the old flower heads to keep the plants blooming.

A number of species of lantana are native to the Southeast; thus they are completely hardy here. They will grow in sun or shade, but sun produces better flowers. They are indifferent to soils and water. About the only problem with lantanas is that they can get weedy, so keep them trimmed to a short, hardy, colorful bush.

Liriope muscari
Liriope

Liriope is a lovely grassy-looking lily that produces blue summer flowers which resemble grape hyacinths. Liriope grows in clumps of about 1 foot high and 18 inches wide. It is frequently used as a low border along walkways, near patios or anywhere a durable short plant is needed. Isolated patches of liriope surrounding a specimen plant or a decorative container are very appealing.

There are variegated, giant, and giant variegated forms. There is also a smaller species, L. spicata, which grows to 8 inches high and wide. This species spreads by underground runners, unlike L. muscari, which you replant by dividing up clumps.

Flowering lantana.

All liriopes are completely hardy here. They'll grow in any soil, in sun or shade, and resist nearly every disease or insect. They are very easy to manage, and this is the primary reason for their extreme popularity.

Grassy leaves of liriope.

Livistona chinensis
Chinese Fan Palm

The Chinese fan palm is unusual among palms in that it remains almost shrub-like, forming a hassock-shaped plant about 6 feet in diameter and 4 feet tall (in the tropics, it gets 25 feet tall). Eventually it will develop a short stem, but the plant never gets huge, which helps if your space is limited.

The Chinese fan palm is another of those easily accommodated plants that prefers sun, moist soil, and occasional feeding. It appears to be hardy throughout our area, but harsh winters will fray and kill the older outer leaves.

The squat growth habit of the Chinese fan palm.

Manihot grahami
Manihot
Cassava
Tapioca Plant

Manihot is a representative of the very important Tapioca genus, of which one member (M. esculenta) is a major food source for people in tropical areas. In the garden manihot forms a lovely round-crowned tree of 15 feet rather quickly. The leaves are palmately lobed and very distinctive. The plant produces inconspicuous flowers all summer.

Manihot does well throughout our area. Most years it is completely hardy, losing only its leaves in the fall. In particularly harsh years it will occasionally freeze back to the ground. When this happens, new plants develop from the trunk, from roots, or from seeds which are freely produced.

Manihot is a very quick grower. With care, they will grow 8 feet a year. Keep the lower branches pruned to prevent crowding. If necessary, you can trim the tops back severely each fall to keep the plants in bounds.

Manihot has nearly all the characteristics of a good tropical. It is fast-growing, insect-free, reasonably hardy, and has interesting foliage. Its only drawback is that the leaves and sap are poisonous. Be careful about planting manihots (and oleanders too) near play areas.

Marsilea sp.
Water Clover

Marsilea is a fern relative that grows in mud and produces 4-leaf-clover-like foliage. The plant is ideal for soggy spots: beside your garden pond, in an isolated depression—anywhere every other groundcover will rot.

Marsilea is hardly an imposing plant, with its little 1-inch 4-parted leaves growing on 3-inch stems. It is hardy everywhere in our area and there are 60 species, nearly all of which are suitable.

Melia azedarach
Chinaberry Tree

This short tree (usually under 20 feet) produces a canopy of parasol-shaped huge fern-like foliage on thick branches. Each spring finds the tree covered with small strange purple and white flowers vaguely reminiscent of orchids. These are followed by clusters of light yellow hard berries about the size of marbles. These attract all kinds of birds throughout the winter.

The only drawback to the chinaberry tree is its exceedingly close foliage that produces a very dense shade. And if you don't like birds, you may find the berries a nuisance.

The chinaberry is tolerant of most soils, is completely hardy everywhere in our zone, and is a very easy-to-grow short tree.

Monstera deliciosa
Split-Leaf Philodendron
Swiss Cheese Plant
Ceriman

Aptly named, the Swiss cheese or split-leaf philodendron is the houseplant with splits in its small leaves and holes and slits in the large ones. Like the pothos, the Swiss cheese plant comes in two forms: juvenile and mature. The juvenile form is very viny and produces leaves 10 to 15 inches long, heart-shaped, and with several slits along each edge. When the mature plant develops, it becomes less viny, producing leaves 30 inches or more in diameter with slits and holes all through them. At maturity, the plant produces a rather fleshy green jack-in-the-pulpit type flower.

The Swiss cheese plant is not hardy in northern parts of zone 9, but it is commonly grown outdoors in the southerly parts of the zone, and it seems to grow without regard for soil or exposure. Naturally, if you provide good soil, fertilizer and water, it will do better, but, like others of this family, it is a very tolerant plant.

The Swiss cheese plant does well near walls, where it can climb. I try to put them in a focal point, since the plant is always attractive.

Musa sp.
Bananas

It would be hard to imagine a tropical garden without banana plants. Bananas, with their huge, droopy leaves, prodigious growth rate, and characteristic tropical fruit, virtually symbolize the tropical garden.

Along the Gulf Coast the common banana, Musa paradisiaca sapientum, seldom produces fruit predictably; however, many find that large clumps of bananas will fruit every couple of years. The problem is that they don't ripen before frost. It seems that each stem on a banana plant lasts 2 to 3 years, towards the end of which a flower shoot is produced, and subsequently, bananas.

If your plant is phasing right, a new shoot will develop in mid-summer of the first year; the shoot will then reach almost full size the second year. In the spring of the third year the stem will produce a few leaves, then flower and fruit quickly enough to have time to ripen through the summer.

The problem is convincing the banana plant not to send up shoots too early or too late. If too early, the banana will bloom at the end of the second year, either just before frost or in spring, but without enough leaves to support the crop. Fall suckers have similar problems. In any case it's doubtful that you will go into production here in the coastal South.

The flowers, whenever they form, are a real curiosity and lend an exotic flare to the garden. After flowering or fruiting, the particular stem will begin to die and should be cut away to make room for the developing young plants that surround the parent. Usually the common banana grows 15 to 20 feet tall and forms a clump up to 6 feet in basal diameter.

Besides the common banana, four other species have much to recommend them and will add a good deal of character to the garden. The first is the pink-flowered Musa rosacea, which grows to about 10 feet tall and puts out flowers that look like the small flowers of the common banana. The plant clusters profusely and produces a striking pink flower in mid-summer. It is ideal for small atriums or tight places where a common banana would overwhelm the position.

Another banana, Musa zebrina, sometimes called the blood banana, ranks as my favorite. It is a slender plant, perhaps 10 to 17 feet tall, and has leaves that are blotched with red on the upper side and all red beneath. This plant is grown only for its foliage; it is a marvelous accent plant and provides a great conversation piece to any garden.

Two other bananas that deserve mention are Musa cavendishii and Musa ensete. M. cavendishii is a dwarf, edible banana which is reputed to grow fruit in a large flower pot. I worry about these claims, but it no doubt would be worthwhile to try one in protected places like atriums, etc. The plant gets 6 to 10 feet tall, has a rather thick trunk, and allegedly produces myriad 6-inch sweet bananas on occasion.

You've probably seen Musa ensete: the banana tree with the red stripe along the midrib of each leaf. In Mexico M. ensete forms a tremendous plant with 20 foot leaves and a short (10-foot) but immense trunk. In our climate, of course, the plant never grows to such a size; but for the gardener interested in experimenting with a different type of banana, this is it. It is not grown for its flowers or fruit. The flower is a huge cabbage-like thing set down in the leaves while the banana fruits are pithy and have large marble-sized black seeds throughout. The leaves, however, are held straight up in the air, blazoned with that distinctive red "racing stripe."

All bananas love water, rich soil, food, light, and warmth. If you give them lots of food and water and trim off the tattered old leaves, your bananas will put on an astounding performance of growth and development. It is really hard to believe their potential growth rates. Even if they freeze to the ground in winter, they will bounce back up the next spring almost without fail. So try them: they are great fun, very easy to grow, and give a splendid, lush tropical effect.

Common banana, left; dwarf banana, right; blood banana, above.

Nandina domestica
Heavenly Bamboo

Nandina is one of those shrubs that looks quite tropical but really isn't. It forms clusters of thin dark stems that eventually grow about 6 feet tall. The evergreen leaves are distinctive, compound leaves composed of small pointed reddish leaflets connected together on long narrow stems.

Nandina is not a bamboo at all but is related to mahonia, or Oregon grape. The plant produces small clusters of yellow flowers followed by conspicuous, very ornamental red berries. Nandina is frequently used in foundation plantings along walls or anyplace an easily managed hardy shrub is desired.

Nandinas are completely hardy in zone 9. They prefer a well drained acidic soil and moisture year 'round. It's important to keep the soil acidic; nandina leaves will turn yellow in alkaline soil.

The lovely berries, evergreen leaves, and graceful form of the plant make it a superb selection for the garden. However, its distinctive form will not mix with all kinds of landscapes, so decide where to plant your nandina before you purchase one.

Nephrolepis exaltata
Boston Fern

Years ago Boston ferns were found in every parlor. Now there is a resurgent interest in this plant, though it appears that parlors seem to have become extinct.

Boston ferns are easily propagated and cared for. In our area they provide us with a hardy basket for sun or shade. The plant will also establish well in the garden, where it can completely colonize an area with its fine runners.

Like so many tropicals, the Boston fern will grow in the sun, but it gets much prettier in shade, where the lovely leaves can get up to 3 feet long and cascade out of a basket or over a garden wall.

A number of variations of this fern are cultivated today. All are rather difficult without a greenhouse, so stick with the common Boston fern.

Nerium oleander
Oleander

Oleanders come from the deserts of the Middle East, and so they are tolerant of extremes. One of many tropical plants that tolerate nearly any soil, oleanders are also tolerant of drought, heat, frost, bugs, automobile pollution, salty sea air, and asphalt paving. They are very popular in the South and throughout warm-temperate to tropical areas.

The plant is commonly used as a large background planting, as a windbreak, and even in median strips along highways. Oleanders come in a variety of flower colors, from red to pink through white and beyond. There are several lovely double-flowered forms and an ornamental variegated form.

Oleanders flower profusely each spring and sporadically through the summer and fall. They require room, sun, and little else. A mature oleander plant regularly reaches 10-15 feet high and equally as wide, clothed in long, slender 8-inch evergreen leaves. The foliage is quite poisonous, so if you have small children, don't plant oleanders.

Nymphaea sp.
Water Lily

Water lilies come in all leaf sizes, from 12 inches in diameter to dwarfs 2 inches in diameter. Flowers come in white, yellow, red, purple, pink, orange and blue. Some flower at night, others during the day. There is, in fact, a water lily for any pool, from 12 inches wide to an entire lake in size.

Depending upon variety, water lilies need water depths of 6 inches to 3 feet. All require full sun and rich soil which is fertilized when they are planted. Usually, they are set in pots or tubs with rich soil and covered over with an inch of rocks to prevent floating of the pot or disturbance by fish.

The plants are divided every two to three years and replanted. Virtually all water lilies are hardy here, so try them—no garden pool would be complete without them.

Here is a list of hardy varieties to look for:

N. helvola (Pygmy Water Lily)—reddish leaves, yellow flowers

N. marliacea rosea—pink flowers

N. Missouri—night-blooming, white flowers

N. somptuosa—fragrant pink flowers

Onoclea sensibilis
Sensitive Fern

Here is another easy-to-grow fern that establishes well in a shaded setting and is completely hardy along the Gulf Coast. Like the cinnamon fern, the sensitive fern is native to all of our coastal states. It, too, prefers damp to wet humus soil and shade.

The name "sensitive fern" comes not from its soft foliage (its foliage is actually rather coarse) nor from its cultural requirements, which are few; rather, the name comes from the fern's extreme sensitivity to frost. One slight frost and the foliage is gone until next spring. Otherwise, the plant is quite hardy and does well throughout our area in wet, shady places.

Ophiopogon japonicus
Monkey Grass

Here is the standby border plant of southern gardens. It forms small evergreen clumps of grass-like foliage that never needs trimming. The plant is used widely to border flower beds, walkways, patios, etc.

Monkey grass is absolutely hardy. It is indifferent to soils, sun, heat, humidity, etc., and it grows well without any real care throughout zone 9. It is propagated by division of the crown into small tufts. The plant works well wherever a small nonaggressive but extremely tolerant groundcover is needed.

Orchidiaceae
Orchids

Orchids are a logical item for the tropical garden. They are the most elegant of tropical flowers and certainly the one flower that comes to mind when tropics are mentioned.

Flowering water lilies.

Most of the popular orchids would be treated as tender accent plants in our area. Nearly all of the intermediate and warm-growing types will grow very easily outdoors from late March to mid-November. These plants thrive on our hot, humid summer days and foggy nights. Nearly all will do well if hung out among the trees in partial shade, watered twice weekly, and fertilized twice monthly with a 30-10-10 fertilizer.

There are a few hardy or half-hardy orchids which will do well outside all year. The most famous of these are the cymbidiums. Cymbidiums are the corsage type orchids you see around Easter time. They are robust, grassy-looking plants that can produce 20 to 50 flowers or more each year. When you begin to look for cymbidiums, you will discover two types: the standard or full-sized and the miniature. Don't fool around with the standard plants. They require a cooling period in the fall to set buds. We seldom have such a period early enough to allow the standards to bloom properly, so stick with the miniature cymbidiums. These are very easy to grow and even out of flower they are highly ornamental.

In the winter, the cattleyas, dendrobiums, phalaenopsis and vandas will need protection from frost and prefer temperatures above 55°, so it is best to move them into the house near a south or east window where the light is bright, or place them in a greenhouse if you have one.

There are a few hardy or half-hardy orchids which will do well outside all year. The most famous of these are the cymbidiums. Cymbidiums are the corsage type orchids. They are robust, grassy-looking plants that can produce 20 to 50 flowers or more each year. When you begin to look for cymbidiums, you will discover two types: the standard or full-sized and the miniature. Don't fool around with the standard plants. They require a cooling period in the fall to set buds. We seldom have such a period early enough to allow the standards to bloom properly, so stick with the miniature cymbidiums. These are very easy to grow and even out of flower they are highly ornamental.

Cymbidiums are planted in a finely ground fir bark mix or other very open medium. They prefer bright light, want to be kept damp and fed frequently with 30-10-10 fertilizer. The plants will stand frost at least to 27°, but when in bud or flower they should be protected below 34°. I usually bring in the cymbidiums if it is going to freeze hard, but in a protected entryway they'd be fine all year. Don't plant them out in the garden: the cymbidium plant will grow very well, but it seems to require pot bound roots to flower properly.

Cattleya orchid.

Other orchids to try in the garden include a few of the epidendrums like E. alatum, E. tampense and others of that group, all of which can be attempted in oak trees in southern parts of our zone. The ground orchid, Bletia hyacinthia, is completely hardy here. Some gardeners have established cattleyas in more southerly and protected parts of our zone. The plants do quite well and will succeed for years in protected areas or during very mild winters. For the casual gardener, the ground orchid is perhaps the best bet; for the zealous gardener, there is room for lots of experimentation.

Osmunda sp.

The genus Osmunda provides us with two temperate-to-subtropical species of ferns that are widely cultivated in contemporary gardens. Both species discussed below are ideally suited to damp, shady positions in the tropical garden where their classic vase shapes may be developed to the fullest.

Both species do well in damp to wet humus ground with an acid pH of 5.5 to 6.0. Both are completely hardy and will naturalize extensively if conditions are favorable. They will take considerable sun but reach their fullest development in shade, where the leaves (fronds) can fully develop and be protected from the wind.

Osmunda cinnamomea
Cinnamon Fern

The cinnamon fern is native throughout the South from Texas to Florida and north to Canada.

In our gardens it establishes well and will form great patches of 2- to 3-foot tall green vase-shaped plants. The plant enjoys damp to wet conditions and is ideally suited to shaded areas with poor drainage.

Osmunda regalis
Royal Fern

The royal fern has a natural distribution similar to the cinnamon fern, but it also ranges into Mexico and South America. It is an altogether spectacular fern that reaches 4 feet tall and spreads as wide. Its fronds are more coarsely lobed than the cinnamon fern's, giving it a totally different character. The plant does well along streams and ponds where it never needs to dry out. Like the cinnamon fern, it is ideal for wet areas with poor drainage. It is not seen as frequently as the other, but it is much more desirable and spectacular.

Cinnamon fern.

Palms

Palms are always an important contribution to the tropical garden. They lend some very sharp, clean lines to an otherwise frequently diffuse and soft texture. In some ways the abrupt nature of their symmetry, especially in the Washingtonias, can be a problem, but careful thought about the associated plantings and possibly substitution of other palms will enhance their effect. There are a variety of palms, from herbaceous shrubs to huge trees, that will succeed here.

Palms are unusual among woody plants in that they do not add wood to their trunk once it has formed. Most trees begin as thin whips that slowly gain in height, stature, and trunk diameter. Palms, on the other hand, develop as a rosette of leaves on the ground. This rosette expands and forms a trunk the full diameter of the mature tree, even though the plant is only a few feet tall and the trunk is not even evident yet.

Once the tree begins to get taller its crown and trunk size will remain about the same diameter throughout its life. It is important to realize this when planting small palms. You should know the mature diameter of the tree when you plant it because the tree will reach its mature diameter on the ground before it starts to grow tall. For example, Washingtonia is often sold as a small plant in 1-gallon containers. If you plant it 3 feet from the sidewalk, you'll have a problem because Washingtonias develop a crown 10-12 feet in diameter. The seedling reaches this full diameter before it starts to grow taller, and removing leaves from one side will do little to help. It may be many years before the tree will be tall enough to be clear of the walkway.

By realizing that the mature trunk size and leaf spread show on young plants, it is possible to take advantage of this fact. You know that a Washingtonia with a very slender 4- or 5-foot stem and a narrow leaf span will always be somewhat stunted because the tree will have a narrow collar that will constrict its future growth.

As another example, the Windmill palm is a smaller palm with a 6- to 10-inch trunk and small crown of leaves. If you buy a healthy one that has a trunk already, and you place it in the garden, you don't have to worry about the palm overgrowing its position to the degree so many other shrubs might. But remember: certain palms cluster profusely. While no stem will get beyond a certain size, the addition of new stems around the base can add substantially to a plant's diameter.

Within reason, there is a palm for nearly every position in your garden. There are many palms that will grow in our area. Fourteen of the more common and hardy species are discussed under their separate genera. It is possible to make an extensive collection of many palms, and there are many avid collectors who have done just that.

Plant Name	Ultimate Height and Width (feet)
Butia capatita (Cocos cocos Australis)	10 x 10
Chamaerops humilis (Mediterranean fan palm)	15 x 15
Arecastrum Romanzoffianum (Cocos plumosa)	30 x 10
Cycas revoluta (Sago palm)	6 x 6
Dioon edule (Dioon)	5 x 5
Livistona chinensis (Chinese fan palm)	6 x 4
Phoenix sp.	
P. canariensis (Ornamental date palm)	20 x 15
P. reclinata (Senegal date palm)	20 x 10
P. roebelenii (Miniature date palm)	8 x 4
Raphis excelsa (Lady palm)	6 x 4
Sabal sp.	
S. mexicana (Mexican fan palm)	20 x 15
S. minor (Dwarf palmetto)	5 x 5
S. palmetto (Palmetto)	15 x 10
Trachycarpus fortunei (Windmill palm)	8 x 5
Washingtonia sp.	
W. filifera	40 x 15
W. robusta	80 x 20

Washingtonia Palm

Lady Palm

Windmill Palm

Date Palm

Parkinsonia aculeata
Palo Verde
Jerusalem Thorn

The green-stemmed thin-leaved palo verde forms a lovely small 20-foot round-crowned tree that casts only light shade. It flowers profusely late each spring with clusters of lovely yellow flowers. Rather surprisingly for a native desert tree, the palo verde is very tolerant of wet soils as well. Thanks to its lovely shape, colorful flowers and foliage, and extreme tolerance, the tree has found wide favor among southern gardeners. The foliage allows sunlight to filter through to the ground, and the tree has a deep root system, so you can plant smaller items beneath.

The palo verde is the definitive plant-it-and-forget-it tree. It will grow in any soil, never needs water in our region, and is completely hardy. It's only requisite is full sun.

Passiflora sp.
Passion Flower

Passion flower is an aggressive fast-growing vine that produces highly ornate flowers and, on some forms, edible fruits. Flowers vary in color from red and blue to purple, but all are highly colored, complex flowers that are more fascinating than beautiful. Passion flowers are widely used as fence coverings; they do well on trellises or wherever they can climb.

Passion flowers are easy to grow. There are many forms, some of which are completely hardy.

The wispy foliage of the palo verde.

All want lots of plant food, partial to full sun, a support of some kind, and rich, well drained soil. They are rank growers, so trim them back each winter to keep their size down. Since they flower on new wood, the trimming will not adversely effect their flowering potential.

Blossom of the passion flower vine.

Persera americana
Avocado

In the tropics of Central and South America the avocado forms a substantial tree. But in much of our area freezes are too frequent to allow the avocado to get too big. In coastal, more southerly areas and in heavily urbanized areas it is possible to grow an avocado to tree size and, with luck, have it bear fruit.

The tree requires lots of sun and rich, well drained soil. It needs protection, too. The south side of a two-story building would be ideal.

The avocado can be trained to a multi-limbed bush by inducing lots of basal branches and removing any that get more than 10-15 feet long. This will make the plant much easier to protect from the cold. It can also be espaliered along a warm south wall, as are apples, pears, peaches, etc.

Philodendron selloum
Selloum Philodendron
Cut-Leaf Philodendron

This is an immensely popular garden plant throughout the Gulf Coast. The huge cut-leaf philodendron forms 6- to 8-foot mounds of leaves in gardens everywhere in our area. They are used as foundation plantings, as backgrounds in entryways, or wherever an imposing plant is desired. They grow well in sun or shade, but partial shade allows fuller development of the immense leaves. The plant is very tolerant of soils but prefers a sandy mix that will allow its cord-like aerial roots to penetrate easily. With suitable water and high-nitrogen fertilizer, the plants will grow at an explosive rate.

Because of their size, selloum philodendrons should be given lots of room; a circular area at least 6 feet in diameter should be reserved for each plant. If you plant them closer, they will simply fight with their neighbors.

The selloum will stand light frosts (to 28°F) without damage to the leaves. Below this they will die back to the stem, but new leaves develop quickly each spring. Occasional severe winters will kill the stems to the ground. Sometimes hard freezes are fatal to single-stemmed plants. To avoid the possibility of a total kill, I always plant multiple-crowned selloums so that the plant will have extra buds and stems at ground level which can develop after a hard freeze.

Philodendron evansii is similar to, and a hybrid of, the selloum philodendron. It produces a plant that is altogether as big as the selloum, but its leaves are very full rather than cut into little fingers like the selloum. Treat P. evansii like P. selloum and it will do very well.

Several other plants are called philodendrons, but these fall into other genera and are found elsewhere in the book.

Selloum philodendron.

Phoenix sp.
Date Palm

The genus Phoenix gives us one of mother nature's most important economic palms. Dates produced by Phoenix dactylifera are a commercially important crop in several areas of the world. The genus Phoenix is also interesting botanically, since it is one of the few palms to develop foliar spines, which are sharp, reduced leaves found at the base of each leaf. All date palm relatives have these spines, which makes it easy to discover whether the palm you are looking at is a date palm or not.

Along the Gulf Coast three date palms are grown: P. canariensis, P. reclinata, and P. roebelenii. The first two are completely hardy here, the third one is hardy only in southern portions of zone 9.

Phoenix canariensis
Canary Island Date Palm
Ornamental Date Palm

This date palm is widely seen through the coastal South, where it has been planted for many years since it is completely hardy. While the plant resembles the true date palm, it does not bear edible dates. The plant is grown only as an ornamental, one frequently sees huge specimens lining driveways, gracing front lawns or planted along the parking strips in front of houses.

Ornamental date palms are huge. They develop thick trunks up to 30 inches in diameter and 20 feet tall, and on top are clusters of the typical palm fronds up to 15 feet long and 2 feet wide. Some specimens develop clustered trunks which add to their size. Such size is not to be overlooked, since the plants grow quickly. Do not plant them at your entrance, next to the fence or along a walkway. Give them room. If you don't, they'll take it anyway. Now you know why old date palms stand alone in the middle of big lawns; they belong there.

Phoenix reclinata
Senegal Date Palm

This palm is similar to the ornamental date palm except that the plant is much more slender in all respects. It, too, develops a 20-foot trunk which sometimes clusters, but it is more slender and produces smaller fronds. This date is less commonly seen and simply looks like a thin ornamental date palm. Its growth requirements are similar to the date palm's, and it is nearly as hardy.

Phoenix roebelenii
Miniature Date Palm

The miniature date palm is certainly the most manageable of the date palms. It slowly develops a 6- to 8-foot stem about 4 inches in diameter and produces miniature palm foliage 2 feet long. The plant is much less hardy than its relatives and needs protection in northern parts of zone 9. It is ideal for entryways, atriums, and narrow places where other palms would never work. It also does well as a tub plant on patios, etc.

Phormium sp.

This genus contains the New Zealand flax, a very uncommon and quite exotic plant. It's like an iris that gets up to 15 feet tall with reddish leaves. The plant really does come from New Zealand, where it is commonly planted as an ornamental. The great fan-shaped masses of foliage are held very erect, making an excellent textured background for gardens near large pools. The plant is treated as a typical exotic, needing a humus sandy soil with even moisture the year 'round.

Canary Island date palm.

Phormium colensoi
New Zealand Flax

This species is seen less frequently than P. tenax (below). It grows 7 to 10 feet tall and bears yellow flowers. Thanks to its more restricted size, I feel it has more landscaping possibilities in atriums, enclosed entryways and smaller gardens.

Phormium tenax
New Zealand Flax

More colorful and taller than P. colensoi, P. tenax is more widely cultivated for its narrow upright red to purple-tinted leaves and red flowers. The plant will get 15 feet tall, developing a very strict, highly ornamental form. There is a lovely and distinctive variegated form also.

Plumeria sp.
Frangipani

Plumerias, or frangipani as the French call them, are famous as the flowers the Hawaiians use to make leis. Plumerias are lovely five-petaled flowers of pink, yellow, red or white, about 3 inches in diameter, and very fragrant. They grow on a short bush with thick branches a couple of feet long and large tapered leaves up to a foot long. The plant is somewhat ungainly looking, but in flower it is stunning.

Plumerias are tender throughout much of our area, and thus they're often treated as tub plants. Each summer they are put in sandy soil and grown in full sun out of doors. In fall all the leaves fall off, leaving the thick stems. At this point keep them rather dry and in the house until spring, when they grow new leaves and can be put back out again. Plumerias are slow-growing, so pick them carefully and don't waste your time on poor ones.

Plumeria alba
White Frangipani

This species is not seen as often as the following one. It produces pure white fragrant flowers each summer and cannot be distinguished from P. rubra when out of flower.

Plumeria rubra
Red, Pink and Yellow Frangipani

Most of the cultivated frangipani are of this species or its variety, acutifolia. They come in a number of colors, including dark red, medium red, pink, yellow, and white with a yellow throat. All are treated the same way. Since there are so many colors, I always try to select the plants when in flower so I know that the plant produces a flower of the form and color I want.

Pothos scandens
Pothos

This is certainly one of the most common of all houseplants. Next to Philodendron cordatum there are probably more pothos sold than any other plant. Pothos are those vines with heart-shaped green leaves streaked with yellow that you see in containers everywhere.

In the warm regions of the Gulf Coast pothos becomes a dynamic outdoor vine. Instead of 4-inch heart-shaped leaves, the outdoor pothos slowly develops huge 12- or 15-inch leaves totally streaked with yellow. The difference is that the houseplants remain juvenile plants while the big-leaf forms are mature. One regularly sees a small-leaved pothos at the bottom of a palm tree connected to a mature pothos half way up.

Pothos is very easy: give it light, water, and fertilizer and it will grow at a terrific rate. In protected areas and southerly portions of our range, a pothos will grow to the top of a palm tree in a few years.

This is another excellent shade plant. It will do well as a ground or wall cover and, given some reasonable care, it will perform beautifully for you and add a colorful touch to your garden.

Punica granatum
Pomegranate

Pomegranates are large apple-shaped fruits that are sour and seedy. In the tropical garden they form a lovely shrub up to 12 feet tall that produces a very exotic double red flower. The fruits develop later (and they need a long hot summer to develop properly). There is also a lovely dwarf form (4 feet tall) that produces lovely double red flowers and miniature fruits.

Both pomegranates are useful as foundation plantings. They are completely hardy and have a minimal requirement of good soil, partial shade to full sun, and plant food to induce more flowering. They are not aggressive shrubs, and they make excellent specimens near entryways, especially the dwarf form.

Plumeria flower, the fragrant blossom the Hawaiians use to make leis.

Plants for Shaded Areas

With so many plants producing cascades of huge leaves, tall stems and massive shadows, what to grow on the ground, and in the shade, becomes an important question. Fortunately, we have a wide variety of shade-loving, or at least shade-tolerant, plants to choose from.

In general, shade plants produce disproportionate large leaves which are held parallel to the ground to catch the light. Most tend to ramble about in search of light and most can grow aggressively when conditions are right. Once established, few are bothered by weeds, falling leaves, etc. Nearly all do better if not disturbed or walked upon, so have your walkways placed where you want to go in the garden. The list of potential candidates is endless, but here are a few suggestions.

Acuba japonica	Gold Dust Plant	Fatsia japonica	Fatsia
Adiantum sp.	Maiden Hair Fern	Ficus pumila	Climbing Fig
Alocasia macrorrhiza	Elephant Ear	Hedra helix	English Ivy
Alsophila australis	Australian Tree Fern	Liriope sp.	Liriope
Aralia papyrifera	Rice Paper Plant	Monstera deliciosa	Split Leaf Philodendron
Asparagus sp.	Asparagus Fern	Nephrolepis exaltata	Boston Fern
Aspidistra sp.	Cast Iron Plant	Ophiopogon sp.	Monkey Grass
Bambusa pygmaea	Dwarf Bamboo	Philodendron selloum	Selloum Philodendron
Caladium bicolor	Caladium	Pothos scandens	Pothos
Chlorophyllum comosum	Spider Plant	Sultana impatiens	Sultana
Coleus blumei	Coleus	Syngonium podophyllum	Nepthytis
Colocasia esculenta	Elephant Ear	Tradiscantia sp.	Wandering Jew
Dicksonia antarctica	Tasmanian Tree Fern		

Raphiolepis indica
Indian Hawthorne

The Indian hawthorne is a very desirable ornamental shrub for the tropical garden. It is useful as a foundation planting, hedge or as a background shrub in front of which shorter tropicals can be planted. The plant is a warm-temperate species from India.

Each spring the bush is completely buried in clouds of beautiful pink flowers; additional flowers are produced sporadically throughout the summer, with a second concentration of blooms in late fall.

Foliage on the Indian hawthorne is dark green, oval-shaped, and about 2 inches long; it is evergreen, giving the shrub special appeal in the winter, when other tropicals are at their dismal worst.

The Indian hawthorne eventually forms a large bush to 6 feet wide, but it grows slowly, adding only a few inches of growth to each branch in the spring.

The plant is very undemanding about soil. Of course, a nice humus loam is best. It prefers full sun, which helps the flowers and gives good color to the foliage. The shrub is hardy throughout our zone and only requires water during our very dry periods.

In addition to the common forms, there is a lovely dwarf Indian hawthorne and an exceptional form (R. indica 'Enchantress') chosen for its compact nature and abundance of bloom.

Raphis excelsa
Lady Palm

The lady palm is a profusely branching small fan palm type from the Orient. It is occasionally used as a hedge plant because it stays short, usually under 6 feet, and can be pruned lightly or kept in bounds by sidewalks. The very dark green, glossy fan-type foliage is a lovely contrast to surrounding plants. Thanks to its smaller size, the plant works well in atriums and elsewhere where a small delicate palm is needed.

The lady palm is sensitive to cold in northern parts of zone 9, but it is completely hardy in the southern parts. The plant does well in partial shade to full sun and needs an open soil and even moisture all year.

Lady palm. This palm stays short and can be used as a hedge.

Rhoeo discolor
Moses in a Boat

Rhoeo is a non-trailing member of the wandering Jew family. In many parts of the country it is a popular houseplant; here in the Southeast it is commonly seen in gardens.

The common rhoeo is a large rosette type plant with 12-inch-long, lance-shaped leaves that are green above and purple below. The plant does well in sun or partial shade, as a border, along walls, or as a specimen planting.

Rhoeo is another easy plant to grow. It prefers sun, which enhances its leaf color and rosette form; any well drained soil is sufficient. Keep it moist.

The name "Moses in a Boat" comes from the way the plant flowers. At maturity, rhoeo produces a series of boat-shaped inflorescences out of which pop one or two three-petaled white flowers. Each flower ("Moses") lasts a day or so but is immediately replaced by another. It's a cute plant that young children like because of its "funny" flowers.

Three other forms of rhoeo are commonly seen: a variegated form, a dwarf clustering form, and a dwarf clustering variegated form. All are easy, but the dwarf forms don't seem to flower often.

Sabal sp.
Palmetto

Sabal, like Washingtonia, is an American palm genus. It is distributed from Florida west to Texas and south into Mexico. Throughout the South, sabals are planted as ornamental plants. The tree palmettos are very distinctive. They have a gray to white trunk topped with palmate leaves. Below these are attached the old leaf bases and petioles that remain for years after the leaves have fallen away.

Palmettos are hardy everywhere in our region and are easy to grow. They are regularly shipped around the South loaded on flat-bed trucks like so many telephone poles. When they reach their destination, the palms are staked up in place where they commence growth again. They seem indifferent to soil type or moisture levels, but prefer sunny locales away from trees. Like other tall palms, they look better planted in groups of three to five.

Sabal Mexicana
Mexican Fan Palm

The Mexican fan palm and the palmetto look similar except the Mexican palm is stockier. It has a trunk up to 18 inches thick and 20 feet tall, topped by a distorted palmate leaf that botanists call "costapalmate." That means there is a slight rib in it, giving each leaf a flexed appearance. The leaves form a top about 15 feet in diameter, sometimes smaller. The plant retains its dead leaf stalks as the palmetto does. It is not seen as frequently as the palmetto, probably because most Mexican fan palms must be imported from Mexico.

Sabal minor
Dwarf Palmetto

One of only a few stemless palms, the dwarf palmetto adds a real tropical look to the garden. It is native to wet places from Texas to Florida. The plant eventually forms a bushy mass about 5 feet tall and wide. It is completely hardy, takes sun or shade, and prefers very wet soil.

Sabal palmetto
Cabbage Palm
Palmetto

Certainly one of our most common and hardy palms, this plant is native to Florida and Georgia, where it is very widespread. It is smaller than the Mexican fan palm, with which it shares its retention of leaf bases and white trunk. The tree produces palmate leaves in a round top about 10-12 feet in diameter.

The tree is very tolerant; it can probably withstand more abuse than any other palm. It likes sun, good soil and occasional watering during droughts. Otherwise it is an easy, interesting palm for the garden.

Salix sp.
Willows

The willow family is in no sense a tropical family, yet the group provides such important background plants that I have included them here. Without exception, all of the members considered here are fast-growing, of sturdy form and easy cultivation. These willows all thrive on water, sun, hot summers and mild winters. They seem indifferent to soil type so long as it is moist. They all get quite large and have extensive shallow root systems which are highly competitive with surrounding plants.

Willow trees are fast growers, up to 6-10 feet a year is not unusual for a healthy young one. As such they are messy, since they are always dropping leaves, twigs, and catkins (flowers) in the spring.

They will propagate from a branch in water, but selected forms must be purchased, of course. I like them, but be aware of their commonly weedy habits and large size. Some people say the roots get into water pipes—a consideration if your plumbing is poor; others say that "weed" trees like willows are "short-lived." My guess is that anyone planting a willow will not be around, by virtue of moving away or some other reason, to see the tree die, so don't worry about it.

Salix babylonica
Weeping Willow

The weeping willow is of course, singular in its shape, with great weepy branches spread 40-60 feet high at maturity and each hanging 10 or more feet. The trees are impressive, but give them room. There are several selected forms, including the Niobe weeping willow and others.

Salix matsudana tortuosa
Corkscrew Willow

The corkscrew willow is really a giant shrub. It's one of those plants you either love or hate. Many feel it is one of nature's really curious plants, with its corkscrew twigs, contorted leaves and intricate branching. Others feel it is a hideous grotesque weed. Anyway, it forms a shrub 15 or so feet tall and about as wide. It tends to die back somewhat in winter, but judicious pruning will remove the dead wood and keep the bush in bounds. Any winter losses are immediately replaced each year, so if you like it, try it.

Stenotaphrum secundatum
Variegated St. Augustine Grass

Variegated St. Augustine grass is the variegated form of our common lawn grass. It really is quite pretty as a hanging basket where it can cascade 3 or 4 feet. Other uses are limited because of its rank growth.

The plant is easy to grow in sun or shade. It needs lots of fertilizer and water, but otherwise it is quite hardy. It grows well from cuttings and withstands heavy shearing to keep its form. Don't try variegated St. Augustine as a groundcover except in limited areas; the effect isn't very dramatic.

Chinch bugs are about the only problem. Occasionally they will attack it just as they attack your lawn; otherwise, it makes a curious addition to your garden.

Strelitzia sp.
Bird of Paradise

One of the most popular and outstanding tropical plants is the bird of paradise, which actually occurs in two forms, the regular and the giant-sized. Both forms are planted regularly in protected locales throughout zone 9.

The birds of paradise are related both to heliconias, with which they share a rather similar flower form, and, more distantly, to bananas, with which they bear some vegetative resemblance.

"Birds" are sensitive to frost and must be protected in the northern parts of our zone. They prefer sandy, acid soil, even moisture, and full sun to flower well.

Both species are very useful in protected entryways, in atriums or wherever these unusual plants can be protected from hard freezes; otherwise it is necessary to treat them as tub plants.

Strelitzia nicolei
Giant Bird of Paradise

The giant bird looks more like a super heliconia than it does a bird of paradise. The plant grows 6 to 8 feet tall, develops a multitude of trunks with two rows of spatulate leaves on top. The flowers are borne in clusters out of the leaf axils. They are rather large, with 10-inch bracts that produce many white petals, a few at a time.

Strelitzia reginae
Bird of Paradise

This is the florists' bird of paradise. It grows on a short 3-foot-high plant that never forms the tree S. nicolei does. The flowers develop singly out of the leaf axils each summer and fall. They are about 6 inches long and produce blue and orange petals. If you provide a sandy soil in a sunny protected locale, it is possible to grow these out-of-doors in all of our zone, but they must be protected from hard frost to survive.

Syngonium podophyllum
Arrowhead Vine
Nepthytis

This species contributes a number of varieties of viny houseplants to the world's gardeners. All forms are vigorous vines with arrowhead-shaped leaves that are either green or variegated in different ways. They adapt to about any soil—they will even grow in water—and many home gardeners manage to successfully grow them in the darkest corners of the house. When placed outdoors near a house or wall, the plants will climb vigorously.

Syngonium does freeze back in cold weather, but it returns in a vigorous way each spring. On walls in protected areas they will remain green all winter.

To properly develop your syngonium, feed and water it heavily. The plant is especially useful in dark corners under densely leafy bushes, planted along walls where they will climb aggressively, or in shady hanging baskets.

Arrowhead vine, a rugged plant that you can use anyplace. It is a strong climber and will quickly cover a wall or trellis.

Tabernamontana divaricata (grandiflora)
Indian Carnation
Carnation of India

This bush rather resembles a small-flowered gardenia. It bears evergreen waxy leaves in pairs and 1- to 2-inch double white "carnations" each spring. The plant will eventually get 6 feet tall in warm areas, but it is sensitive to hard freezes and needs protection in northern parts of our zone.

The plant does well in sun or partial shade. It needs moisture year 'round and an acid, humus soil. It's one of many lovely shrubs for foundation plantings along walkways, in atriums or protected entryways. It is very ornamental in or out of flower and is a valuable piece in any tropical garden.

Trachelospermum jasminoides
Confederate Jasmine

Hardly a tropical, but nevertheless useful and beautiful, the confederate jasmine is an excellent evergreen vine that is clothed in fragrant white flowers each spring. The plant comes in two forms: a tall climbing version and a groundcover version (T. jasminoides pubescens). Their uses are obvious. The difference between them is that the climber flowers and climbs well, while the groundcover form is a weak trailing plant that only flowers after several years. There are a couple of forms of variegated confederate jasmine, too.

Cultivation of this plant is easy. It is completely hardy, likes a moist soil, sun or shade and little else. It does well with little attention but should be pruned frequently or else it will take over the garden.

Trachycarpus fortunei
Windmill Palm

The Windmill palm is desirable for a number of reasons. The plant is completely hardy, is very compact in stature, and has a very distinctive trunk. It produces blunt-tipped palmate leaves forming a crown about 5 feet in diameter. The trunk is slender, up to 8 feet tall, perhaps 10 inches in diameter, and completely covered with a burlap-like fiber which is highly ornamental and distinctive.

Cultivation is easy: the plant seems impartial to soil so long as it is damp and slightly acid. It does well in full sun or partial shade. Its easily met requirements, engaging form, and trim size make it a delight in any tropical garden.

The windmill palm is very easy to grow. It is naturally compact, growing to 8 feet tall.

Vitex agnus-castus
Chaste Tree

Vitex is a lovely small tree or large bush with gray-green palmate foliage and dusty blue flowers in late summer. Its small size and lovely summer flowers endear it to gardeners who want a small colorful tree or bush that requires little care.

Vitex is completely hardy here. It requires full sun, sandy soil, and prefers to be kept dry.

It is extremely useful as a screen, windbreak or foundation planting. The plant never gets unmanageably large, nor does it choke out its neighbors.

Washingtonia sp.

The two species of fan palm, W. filifera and W. robusta, are commonly grown throughout the South. They are very similar in habit and culture, thus many people regularly confuse the two. Both are hardy everywhere in zone 9, but W. filifera is more hardy than W. robusta.

Like other palms, the Washingtonias reach full diameter before they begin to grow taller. Realizing this will help you avoid overcrowding problems near walls, driveways, etc.

Washingtonias are regularly used as windbreaks, parkway plantings, etc. The plants are fairly hardy, withstanding freezes to 20°, prolonged drought, and excessive rain and heat without problems. This is not really surprising, since Washingtonias are native to the deserts of Mexico and the southwestern United States, where they grow along the few streams of those regions.

Washingtonia filifera
Fan Palm

W. filifera is differentiated from the other species by its very heavy trunk, sometimes 30 inches in diameter, and the long filaments that occur on each fan-shaped leaf. The entire plant is very stocky in appearance, with a huge head of leaves, a large thatch of dead leaves below, and the rather squat-like form. W. filifera is the hardier of the two species. It grows up to 40 feet or more, with at least a 15-foot leaf span from side to side.

Washingtonia robusta
Fan Palm

This fan palm is the faster growing of the two. It produces a slender trunk with a tapered base that grows much taller than filifera does. Also, the leaves have fewer filaments on them. It is somewhat less hardy, so the filifera may be a safer bet. At maturity robusta can reach 80 feet tall with a trunk diameter of 1 foot to 18 inches.

A young Washingtonia filifera. This is the best choice for a tall palm tree—it grows up to 40 feet tall. Although W. Robusta grows to 80 feet, it is not as cold hardy as filifera.

Yucca aloifolia
Yucca
Spanish Bayonet

This yucca provides us with a lovely erect stiff-leaved complement to the tropical garden. Each plant forms a cluster of stems up to 6 feet tall. Each stem is covered with long, narrow, upraised, curving green spine-tipped leaves about 1 foot long, 2 inches wide. Each spring the plant produces a head of bell-shaped white waxy flowers about 2 inches long. The plant is highly ornamental and is extremely useful near garden lamps, in dry corners, or as a clustered specimen planting.

Cultivation is easy: yuccas prefer a dry soil, lots of sun, and little else. Do not crowd other plants around it and don't put it too near traffic areas, unless you want everyone to get punctured.

Zantedeschia sp.
Calla Lily

Calla lilies are not lilies at all but are members of the philodendron family. They have been grown for years as summertime bulbs throughout the United States.

Callas are planted out in the spring in a very sandy soil with good moisture. Since they are grown for their flowers, they require nearly full sun. They also prefer a lower-nitrogen fertilizer than others of the philodendron family. A 5-10-5 or 6-10-4 fertilizer is very good. All require lots of moisture.

Like the caladiums, they die down in the fall, but unlike them, callas don't have to be dug up each fall. In fact, they will develop into large plants if left undisturbed. There are three species of calla seen frequently in our gardens.

Zantedeschia aethiopica
White Calla Lily

The most famous calla is the white calla lily. It produces triangular leaves on 30-inch stems, and the flowers develop above these. In Mexico, they are commonly planted along streams where they develop in great profusion and are cut to supply the cut flower trade there. In our area they are frequently planted in protected situations and are allowed to develop, without disturbance, into large plants over the years.

Zantedeschia elliotiana
Yellow Calla Lily

The yellow form is smaller and easier to grow. It also produces triangular leaves ornamented with white spots. The flowers are a butter yellow and are produced on stems about 18 inches tall. This plant can be grown like the white form and seems a bit hardier.

Zantedeschia rehmannii
Dwarf Pink Calla Lily

The dwarf pink calla grows green lanceolate leaves about 15 inches long and produces small 3-inch pink callas on 12-inch stems. This plant is winter hardy in our area, but I try to give it lots of sand so the bulb won't rot in the winter. This calla does well in borders, mixed with other short tropicals. I would not plant a whole bed of these, however, because they're rather nondescript when out of flower.

Index

Index to Botanical Names

Acalypha wilkesiana, 33
Adiantum capillis-veneris, 33
Aechmea sp., 43
Agapanthus sp.
    A. albidus, 34
    A. orientalis, 34
Agave sp.
    A. americana, 34
    A. attenuata, 35
Albizzia julibrissin, 35
Alocasia macrorrhiza, 52
Aloe vera, 35
Alpinia speciosa, 36
Alsophila australis, 36
Amaryllis hallii, 62
Aralia papyrifera, 36
Araucaria sp.
    A. araucana, 37
    A. bidwillii, 37
    A. excelsa, 37
Arecastrum Romanzoffianum, 37
Arundinaria pygmaea, 40
Asparagus sp.
    A. plumosus, 38
    A. retrofractus, 38
    A. sprengeri, 38
    A. sprengeri c.v. meyeri, 38
Aspidistra elatior, 39

Bambusa sp.
    B. glaucescens, 40
    B. ventricosa, 40
Bambusaceae, 39
Bauhinia sp.
    B. corniculata, 42
    B. forficata, 42
Beloperone guttata, 42
Billbergia nutans, 43
Bletia hyacinthia, 71
Bougainvillea sp., 42
Bromelia balansae, 43
Bromeliaceae, 42
Brunfelsia calycina, 44
Butia capitata, 44

Cactaceae, 44
Caladium bicolor, 45
Callisia elegans, 52
Callistemon citrinus, 46
Canna indica, 46
Carica papaya, 47
Carissa grandiflora, 47
Casurina equisetifolia, 47
Catalpa speciosa, 48
Cattleya sp., 71
Ceratostigma plumbaginoides, 48
Cereus peruvianus, 45
Chamaerops humilis, 48
Chlorophytum comosum, 48
Cinnamonum camphora, 48
Citrus sp.
    C. limon, 49
    C. mitis, 49
    C. reticulata, 50
Codiaeum variegatum, 50
Coleus blumei, 50
Colocasia esculenta, 51
Commelinaceae, 50
Cortaderia sellowiana, 52
Cycas revoluta, 53
Cymbidium sp., 71
Cynara scolymus, 53
Cyperus sp.
    C. alternifolia, 53
    C. papyrus, 54
Cyrtomium falcatum, 54

Dendrobium sp., 71
Dicksonia antarctica, 54
Dioon edule, 55
Dioscorea sp.
    D. bulbifera, 55
    D. macrostachya, 56

Epidendrum sp.
    E. alatum, 71
    E. tampense, 71
Epiphyllum ackermannii, 44
Epiphyllum pumilum, 45
Epiphyllum strictum, 45
Eriobotrya japonica, 56
Erythrina crista-galli, 56
Eucalyptus
    E. pulverulenta, 57
Euphorbia pulcherrima, 57

Fatsia japonica, 58
Ficus sp.
    F. carica, 58
    F. decora, 59
    F. pumila, 59
Firmiana simplex, 59
Fortunella margarita, 50

Gardenia jasminoides, 59
Gerbera jamesonii, 59
Graptopetalum paraguayense, 60

Hedera sp.
    H. canariensis, 60
    H. helix
Hedychium coronarium, 60
Heliconia sp.
    H. angustifolia, 61
    H. humilis, 61
    H. rostrata, 61
Hibiscus rosa-sinensis, 61
Hippeastrum striatum, 62
Hymenocallis sp., 62

Impatiens sultani, 64

Jacobinia carea, 65

Koelreuteria sp.
    K. bipinnata, 65
    K. paniculata, 65

Lagerstroemia indica, 65
Lantana camara, 66
Liriope muscari, 66
Livistona chinensis, 67

Manihot sp.
    M. esculenta, 67
    M. grahami, 67
Marsilea sp., 67
Melia azedarach, 67
Mimosa, 35
Monstera deliciosa, 68
Musa sp.

M. cavendishii, 68
M. ensete, 68
M. paradisica sapientum, 68
M. rosacea, 68
M. zebrina, 68

Nandina domestica, 69
Neoreglia sp., 43
Nephrolepis exaltata, 69
Nerium oleander, 70
Nymphaea sp.
  N. Helvola, 70
  N. marliocea, 70
  N. 'Missouri', 70
  N. sumptuosa, 70

Onoclea sensibilis, 70
Ophiopogon japonicus, 70
Opuntia ficus-indica, 70
Orchidaceae, 70-71
  Bletia, 71
  Cattleya, 71
  Dendrobium, 71
  Epidendrum, 71
  Phalaenopsis, 71
  Vanda, 71
Osmunda sp.
  O. cinnamomea, 71
  O. regalis, 72

Parkinsonia aculeata, 73
Passiflora sp., 73

Persea americana, 74
Phalaenopsis sp., 71
Philodendron sp.
  P. evansii, 74
  P. selloum, 74
Phoenix sp.
  P. canariensis, 75
  P. reclinata, 75
  P. roebelenii, 75
Phormium sp.
  P. colensoi, 76
  P. tenax, 76
Plumeria sp., 41, 76
  P. alba, 76
  P. rubra, 76
Pothos scandens, 76
Pumica granatum, 77

Raphiolepis indica, 78
Raphis excelsa, 79
Rhoeo discolor, 79

Sabal sp.
  S. Mexicana, 79
  S. minor, 80
  S. palmetto, 80
Salix sp.
  S. babylonica, 80
  S. matsudana tortuosa, 80
Sasa veitchii, 40
Setcreasea purpurea, 52
Stenotaphrum secundum, 80

Strelitzia sp., 80-81
  S. nicolei, 81
  S. reginae, 81
Syngonium podophyllum, 81

Tillandsia sp.
  T. baileyi, 43
  T. recurvata, 43
  T. usneoides, 43
Tabernamontana divaricata (grandiflora), 81
Trachelospermum jasminoides, 81
Trachycarpus fortunei, 82
Tradiscantia fluminensis, 52
Trichocereus peruvianus, 45

Vanda sp., 71
Vitex angus-castus, 82

Washingtonia sp.
  W. filifera, 82
  W. robusta, 82

Xanthosoma sagittifolium, 51

Yucca aloifolia, 83

Zantedeschia sp.
  Z. aethopica, 83
  Z. elliotiana, 83
  Z. rehmannii, 83
Zebrina pendula, 52

Index to Common Names

aechmeas, 43
agapanthus, 34
agave, 34
air potato, 55
Algerian ivy, 60
allamanda, 35
amaryllis, 62
araucaria, 37
arrowhead vine, 81
artichoke, 53
asapargus fern, 38
Australian pine, 47
Australian tree fern, 36
aucuba japonica, 33
avocado, 74

bamboo, 39, 41
  Buddha's belly, 40
  clumping, 40
  heavenly, 69
  hedge, 40
  kuma grass, 40
  Pygmy, 40
  running, 40

bananas, 41, 68
  blood, 68
  common, 68
  dwarf, 68
  pink-flowered, 68
bauhinia, 42
bird of paradise, 80-81
blood banana, 68
blue lily of the Nile, 34
Boston fern, 69
bottle brush, 46
bougainvillea, 42
bromeliads, 42, 43
Buddha's belly bamboo, 40
bunya bunya, 37
bushes
  bottlebrush, 46
  corkscrew willows, 80
  crapemyrtle, 65
  fatsia, 58
  frangipani, 76
  gardenia, 59
  hibiscus, 61
  Indian carnation, 81

  lantana, 66
  oleander, 70
  pomegranate, 77
  tapioca, 67
  yucca, 83
butterfly ginger, 60

cabbage palm, 80
cactus
  dwarf orchid, 45
  mission pear, 44
  orchid, 44, 45
  queen of the night, 45
  torch, 45
caladiums, 45
calamondin orange, 49
calla lily, 83
camphor tree, 48
cannas, 46
carnation of India, 81
cassava, 67
cast iron plant, 39
catalpa, 48
century plant, 34

ceriman, 68
chaste tree, 82
chinaberry tree, 67
Chinese fan palm, 67
Chinese parasol tree, 59
cinnamon fern, 71
cocos australis, 44
cocos plumosa, 37
coleus, 50
confederate jasmine, 81
copper plant, 33
coral bush, 56
coral tree, 56
corkscrew willow, 80
crapemyrtle, 65
creeping fig, 59
croton, 50
cut-leaf philodendron, 74
cyperus, 41

date palm, 75
dioon, 55
dusky rose, 60
dwarf banana, 68
dwarf orchid, 45
dwarf palmetto, 80
dwarf pink calla, 83

edible fig, 58
Egyptian paper plant, 54
elephant ears, 41, 51
elephant's foot, 56
English ivy, 60
eucalyptus, 56

fancy-leaved caladiums, 45
fan palm (see palms)
fatsia, 58
ferns, 34, 41
   asparagus, 38
   Australian tree, 36
   Boston, 69
   cinnamon, 71
   holly, 54
   maidenhair, 33
   sensitive, 70
   sprengeri, 38
   Tasmanian tree, 54
fig, 58
fingernail plant, 43
foxtail sprengeri, 38
frangipani, 76
friendship plant, 43

gardenia, 59
giant bird of paradise, 81
ginger
   butterfly, 60
   shell, 36
gold dust plant, 39

golden raintree, 65
grass
   kuma bamboo grass, 40
   monkey grass, 70
   variegated St. Augustine grass, 80
green wandering jew, 52
gum tree, 56

heavenly bamboo, 69
hedge bamboo, 40
heliconia, 61
hen and chicken, 60
hibiscus, 61
holly fern, 54

impatiens, 64
Indian carnation, 81
Indian hawthorne, 78
Ivy, 60
   Algerian, 60
   English, 60

jacobinia, 65
Japanese varnish tree, 59
jasmine, confederate, 81
jelly palm, 44
Jerusalem thorn, 73

Kuma bamboo grass, 40
kumquat, 40

lady palm, 79
lantana, 66
lemon, 49
lily
   calla, 83
   canna, 46
   lily of the Nile, 34
   spider lily, 62
   water lily, 70
liriope, 66
loquat, 56

maidenhair fern, 33
manihot, 41, 67
medicinal aloe, 35
Mediterranean fan palm, 48
Mexican fan palm, 79
meyer lemon, 49
mimosa, 35
miniature date palm, 75
miniature orange, 49
mission pear, 44
monkey grass, 70
monkey puzzle tree, 37
Moses in a boat, 79

Nagami kumquat, 50
nandina, 69
natal plum, 47

neoregelias, 43
nephthytis, 81
New Zealand flax, 75
Norfolk Island pine, 37

oleander, 70
orange, 49
orchid cactus, 44, 45
orchids, 70
   Bletia, 71
   Cattleya, 71
   Cymbidium, 71
   Dendrobium, 71
   Epidendrum, 71
   Phalaenopsis, 71
   Vanda, 71
orchid tree, 42
osmunda, 71

palms, 41, 72
   cabbage, 80
   Chinese fan, 67
   date, 75
   dwarf palmetto, 80
   fan, 82
   lady, 79
   Mediterranean fan, 48
   Mexican fan, 80
   miniature date, 75
   palmetto, 79
   sago, 53
   Senegal date, 75
   washingtonia, 72
   windmill, 82
palmetto, 79, 80
palo verde, 73
pampas grass, 52
papaya, 47
passion flower, 73
philodendron
   cut-leaf, 74
   selloum, 74
   split-leaf, 68
pine
   Australian, 47
   Norfolk Island, 37
pink-flowered banana, 68
plumbago, 48
plumeria, 41, 76
poinsetta, 57
pomegranate, 77
ponderosa lemon, 49
pothos, 76
purple heart, 52
Pygmy bamboo, 40
Pygmy water lily, 70

queen of the night, 45

rice paper plant, 36, 41
royal fern, 72

rubber tree, 59

sabal palm, 79
sago palm, 53
satsuma orange, 50
selloum philodendron, 41, 74
Senegal date palm, 75
sensitive fern, 70
shell ginger, 36
shrimp plant, 42
silver dollar eucalyptus, 57
Spanish bayonet, 83
spider lily, 62
split-leaf philodendron, 68
sprengeri fern, 38
St. Augustine grass, variegated, 80
striped inch plant, 52
sultana, 64
Swiss cheese plant, 68

tapioca, 67
Tasmanian tree fern, 54
tillandsia, 43
torch cactus, 45
Tansvaal daisy, 59
trees
   Australian pine, 47
   avocado, 74

bunya-bunya, 37
camphor, 48
catalpa, 48
chaste, 82
chinaberry, 67
citrus, 49
coral, 56
eucalyptus, 56
fern, 36, 54
fig, 58
golden rain, 65
mimosa, 35
monkey puzzle, 37
Norfolk Island pine, 16
orchid, 42
palms (*see* palms)
palo verde, 73
parasol, 59
rubber, 59
varnish, 59
willow, 80

umbrella plant, 53

variegated airplane plant, 48
variegated spider plant, 48
variegated St. Augustine grass, 80
vines

allamanda, 35
arrowhead, 81
bougainvillea, 42
confederate jasmine, 81
ivy, 58
nephthytis, 81
passion flower, 73
philodendron, 68
pothos, 76

wandering jew, 52
washingtonia palm, 72, 82
water clover, 67
water lily, 70
weeping willow, 80
white calla, 83
white frangipani, 76
white lily of the Nile, 34
white orchid tree, 42
willow
   corkscrew, 80
   weeping, 80
windmill palm, 72, 82

yellow calla, 83
yesterday today and
   tomorrow, 44
yucca, 83

Subject Index

acid soil, 11
air layering, 15
alkaline soil, 11
aphids, 12
atriums, 25
   cover, 27
   lighting, 25
   plans, 26

beds, 11
black rot, 13
bridges, 32

clay soils, 10
climate
   Gulf Coast, 4-8
   tropical, 1-4
cloud forest, 3
cockroaches, 12
cold, 16
compost, 10
corner garden, 24
cultinars, 16
cuttings, 14

design, 22-23
diseases
   black rot, 13
   rust, 13
   viruses, 13
division, 13
drought, 7, 20

elevated beds, 11
entryways, 25
exposure, 22

fences, 32
fertilizer, 11
fish, 29, 31
focal points, 32
forests
   cloud, 3
   tropical, 2
   tropical deciduous, 3
frost, 7
furniture, 32

garden design, 22-32
garden pools, 29, 31

Gulf Coast climate, 4-7
   vs. tropical climates, 5-6

hardiness, 21
heat, 20
   heat islands, 7
humus, 10

insecticides, 12
insects (see pests)

landscaping (see also: atriums, entryways, garden design), 22-32
layering, 15
leaf rollers, 12
leaves, 10
light, 22
lighting (electric), 32

mature sizes, 23, 33
mealy bugs, 12
montane rain forest, 2-3
mulching, 16
multiple-crowned plants, 16

non-tropical forests, 4

pathways, 24, 29
   atriums, 27
   gardens, 29
patios, 27
peat moss, 10
pests, 12
pill bugs, 12
pine needles, 10
planning, 23
   atriums, 26
planters, 27
plant hardiness, 21
planting, 11-12
pools, 29-31
potted plants, 28
propagation, 13-15
protected entryways, 25
protected plantings, 17

rain, 17
rain forests
   montane, 2
   tropical, 2

raised beds, 24
red spider, 12
rice hulls, 10
runners, 14
rust, 13

sand, 10
screens, 32
seasonal variations
   droughts, 7
   freezes, 7
seeds, 14-15
shade plants, 77-78
slugs, 12
snails, 12
soil
   amendments, 10
   clay, 10
   composition, 9
   drainage, 17
   humus, 10
   mix, 15
   pH, 9, 11
   preparation, 9
   tropical, 2
sow bugs, 12
spacing, 11
sun, 22
swimming pools, 28

temporary structures, 15
tender plants (list), 21
tropics
   climate, 1-4
   location of, 1
   plant habitats, 2-3

variegated plants, 63
viruses, 13

walls, 24, 32
water, 10-11
waterfalls, 29
weather, 5-8
white fly, 12
winter protection, 16-19
wood lice, 12